DOING LIFE DIFFERENTLY

THE ART *of* LIVING
with IMAGINATION

LUCI SWINDOLL

THOMAS NELSON
Since 1798

NASHVILLE DALLAS MEXICO CITY RIO DE JANEIRO

Published in Nashville, Tennessee, by Thomas Nelson.
Thomas Nelson is a registered trademark of Thomas Nelson, Inc.

Thomas Nelson, Inc., titles may be purchased in bulk for educational, business, fund-raising, or sales promotional use. For information, please e-mail SpecialMarkets@ThomasNelson.com

Unless otherwise indicated, Scripture quotations are from the The Holy Bible, New International Version (NIV). © 1973, 1978, 1984, International Bible Society. Used by permission of Zondervan Bible Publishers.

Other Scripture references are from the following sources:
The Message (MSG), © 1993. Used by permission of NavPress Publishing Group.

Library of Congress Cataloging-in-Publication Data Available

ISBN 978-1-4002-0276-8

Printed in the United States of America

10 11 12 13 14 RRD 9 8 7 6 5 4 3 2 1

Photographs and drawings throughout the book by Luci Swindoll.

Pablo Picasso, "Weeping Woman," 1937, © 2002 Estate of Pablo Picasso/Artists Rights Society (ARS), New York.

Dedication

This book is dedicated,
with love and appreciation
to my family,
who encouraged me to
look at life differently . . . and to live it that way.
In effect, they set eternity in my heart.

three years, sans furlough, with the Navy as aerial gunner. He's home on leave now at 6611 99th St, Forest Hills, L. I.

St. Forest Hills
N. Y.
Mar.
1943

Lucille Swindoll

PHOTOGRAPH UNAVAILABLE

AIR MAIL

Contents

Foreword

THE ART OF LIVING WITH IMAGINATION

It was January 14, 1978, and Ney Bailey and I had been invited to Luci Swindoll's home for dinner that Saturday night. Because we were living in the mountains of San Bernardino, California at the time, and Luci's home was in Fullerton . . . a couple hours away . . . she suggested we come for dinner, spend the night, and go to the church her brother pastored. I had met Luci only once before and had fallen in love with her immediately. I had never heard of her brother.

We pulled up in front of her apartment complex, across the street from an elementary school. It was a very unassuming, tiny unit that housed four apartments including hers. I had loved my first encounter with Luci a month or two earlier, found her fascinating, a great storyteller, and very funny. But as I walked up to that little apartment door, I had no idea how my life was about to change . . . in a million ways.

My first impression was hearing gorgeous classical music through the front door screen as we rang the doorbell. Then we entered the small living room, which was a combination library, art gallery, symphony hall, and very warm and inviting little conversational area. The walls were lined with a gorgeous collection of leather-bound books (resting on rough-hewn boards on cinder blocks) and original art. It was almost the tiniest apartment I'd ever seen and maybe the most dramatic room I'd ever entered.

That night was a turning-point in my life. Marilyn Meberg joined us for dinner, and we had the most amazing conversations. The next morning I heard Chuck Swindoll teach from the Book of Acts. (*WHO is your brother?* I remember asking Luci!) After church, when Marilyn dropped by to say good-bye to us, we all took out our calendars to determine the next time we'd get together. At the time, all four of us were managing full lives and obligations, so we spent the last part of our visit together putting the next date on our calendars. We did that with every visit for probably twenty years. (FINALLY, we've moved into the same neighborhood, go to the same

"My Girl"

A little corner with ...
A little mug, a spoon, ...
... bears in ...
... ring to ...
... ll letter ...
... to resou ...
..., See! S...
... ix outstr...
... ir, A little u...

a little dol...   ... little pair
little dre...   ... little teac...
little sch...   ... little grad...
little stu...   A little ch...
little coat, ...   A little escor...
little while to play and bow, A little ...
little party somewhat late, A little ling...
little walk in leafy June, A little tal...
little ceremony grave, A little struggle ...
little cottage on a lawn, A little kiss My ...

church, work in the same ministry, and constantly leave one another with the same phrase, *"See you in twenty minutes."*)

If I've learned anything about Luci Swindoll, it's that she lives life differently. She lives the life out of every day. She's done that all her life and the difference it's made is remarkable, not just for her own life but for every life she touches. Her life reminds me of John 10:10 when Jesus himself said, "I have come that you might have life, and have it more abundantly." She enjoys the abundant life and she invites us to enter into that joy. Having known her so well and so long, I know that what she enjoys is not an abundance of things. It's an abundance of life.

She now spends her weekends ministering to women as a speaker for Women of Faith and races home on Saturday nights or in the wee hours of Sunday morning to hear her brother at our church in the neighborhood. She spends her weeks enjoying the fruit, both tangible and intangible, of a life well lived, choices well made, and the bounty and generosity that comes from the hand of the God she's loved all her life.

To be sure, Luci Swindoll understands the art of living with imagination more than anyone I know. And she's more than willing to mentor and lead anyone along that path of God-given freedom. She's done it with me and dozens of my personal friends to whom I've said at one time or another, "You have to meet Luci." She's done it for thousands more both directly and indirectly (through her writing and speaking). She knows how to live and how to teach others. In her indomitable style, she'll teach anyone, anything . . . anywhere. Not because she's so eager to teach but because she finds those who are teachable so irresistible.

In our relationship with God, is there any limit to our becoming all he created us to be? Luci Swindoll would say no. Can we really make our way through the challenges of life with an open heart to learn and grow, not regretting the past nor fearing the future? Luci Swindoll would say yes. And, after reading this book, I believe you will agree.

—Mary Graham
President, Women of Faith
March 2010

CANON AE 1

w/24 m r
(wide angl

CAPTURING THE JOURNEY

PART 1

PART 1

The Masai village lay about two miles from our tent, on the Mara River in the Serengeti. You got there by the seat of your pants. Well, almost. That Land Rover was at least twelve years old, with dirty, gray upholstery hanging in fringes from the ceiling, and as we bumped along, I was being bruised on every part of my old, tired body.

This place was literally right out of nowhere. Here an entire culture carried on their lives day after day—eating, drinking, marrying, conducting enterprise, raising their children, and burying their dead. They didn't have cars or phones or one single modern convenience, yet they were happy as larks.

The Masai, Kenya's most famous tribe, are a proud, strikingly beautiful people who enjoy harmony with the land, believing God gave them all the cows in the world and the wild animals belong to him and cannot be harmed. They live in huts made of mud and cow dung and exist on a diet of milk, maize, and blood extracted from their cattle (which they rarely use for meat).

This particular village covers roughly a square city block, with huts laid out in a circle. Daily life takes place in the middle of the circle. All their wares are spread out on a big rug—beads, jewelry, souvenirs—and everything is for sale, with price tags attached. I bought a tiny little beaded pot held together by wire, which now sits on my desk, and a bracelet made of the hair from a giraffe's tail. I also purchased two wooden batons made from the African olive tree: one lined with colorful beads, used by the chief in ruling the tribe; the other, a sort of all-purpose polished stick for beating off an enemy or kneading bread, whichever was the more pressing at the time.

I asked the guy who let us in if I could take pictures, and he assured me I could "for a price." The women lined up, adorned in their customary beads and jewelry and bright red cloaks tied together at the shoulder. Some were holding their babies or grandbabies. Flies swarmed all over them, to which they paid no mind, and none of them objected to the photos I took. It was, for me, a "Kodak moment."

With every passing minute, my dear friend and traveling companion Mary Graham was suggesting we leave. "Let's just get back in the car and get outta here, Luci. I can't bear to see these children with flies in their eyes and mouths. And can't you smell that dung? Doesn't it make you sick to your stomach? We've got to hurry or I may throw up."

After walking around the compound and into various huts, chatting with our guide, the chief, and several of the women, I reluctantly put away my camera, paid the man who let us in, shook hands with everyone, and said good-bye.

As we bumped down the rutted path and I snapped pictures through the back window, Mary said, "I'm so glad we left, Luci. I just hate to think how those people have to live." But I was thinking, *I could have spent the day there.* Everything was so interesting . . . foreign to all I know and how I live and where I'm from. What an adventure. In my heart I felt almost at home. (I don't know how it would have been at dinnertime or bedtime, but I can imagine.) There was a sense of homeostasis—a feeling of equilibrium among complete strangers. I didn't feel like a stranger. Yet nothing about that place could have been more unusual or more different from all I know.

Why am I like this? Why is adventure so appealing to me? Why is Mary's response like that of almost everyone I know, while I am the one who loves the risk, takes the chance, doesn't want to miss anything out of the ordinary—even dangerous at times—on the journey of life?

The answer to these questions was set in motion many years ago.

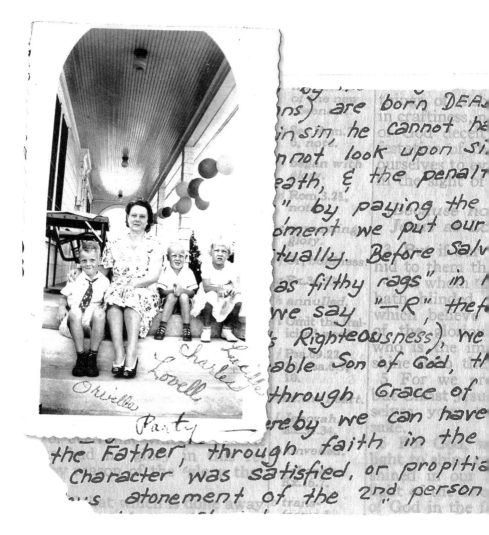

My father gave me my first road map—the way to Momo's. At the end of the journey, he had drawn a picture of her house, a large, two-story, white wooden frame with tall columns on a big front porch. I loved that house, and I loved my grandmother. She could do everything. Play the piano like a house afire, sing, laugh, encourage and lift my spirits when nobody else could. When we came to visit, there was always cold pop in the refrigerator and Momo's arms were open to greet us.

My family lived in Houston, Texas, at the time, and I remember going to El Campo to visit when I was eight years old. World War II had just started, and Daddy had a 1941 Ford. He drove, Mother sat beside him, and we three kids lollygagged in the backseat. My older brother, Orville, was nine; my younger brother, Chuck, was six; and I was the eight-year-old girl in the middle. The Swindoll kids: Bubba, Tutta, and Babe. On many of those trips, we stood on the floorboard of the backseat right behind Mother and Daddy (driving them crazy probably), waiting for the first glimpse of El Campo's "skyline"—a big cotton gin. Whichever one of us said aloud, "First one to see El Campo" got a nickel from Daddy. This, of course, caused us to stay quiet and watch the horizon. That nickel was a great reward.

We had lived in El Campo before moving to Houston. On Saturdays, the three of us went to the Normana Theater and spent the afternoon. Daddy gave each of us a quarter, which bought a hamburger for a nickel, a Coke for a nickel, a bag of popcorn for a nickel, and the movie for a nickel. We always gave a nickel back to Daddy as change—maybe the same nickel he gave us for seeing El Campo first.

And the movie wasn't just a movie. It was Disneyland before there was one! We saw a double feature (Westerns, usually), cartoons, two serials, and RKO News. Sometimes there was even a live talent show. Afterward we rode imaginary horses all the way home across the lawns of neighbors, clacking out mouth noises as horse hooves stomped the grass, holding tightly to the reins so they wouldn't get away from us. Worn out by the long ride, we'd flop down on the bed when we got home or stop by Momo's for a cold pop. Often she was playing the piano when we got there or working in one of her dozens of scrapbooks, pasting in black-and-white photos or articles she had cut out of newspapers or magazines.

Momo and I talked often about life, the little things that mattered to her and to me. I would tell her my problems or concerns, and she would say, "Let's sing. You take the melody, and I'll take the harmony." I didn't want to

sing—I wanted to pout. So she'd let me pout awhile then fix a sandwich and cold drink and tell me something funny about a neighbor or somebody in the family, and before long I kind of forgot my problem and we'd sing. Usually a hymn or something patriotic. Maybe a campfire tune. In the middle of our rendition, she often got up from her chair, went to the piano, motioning for me to follow (not missing a note), and started playing in the key in which we were singing. We'd stay there for maybe an hour. Singing and singing and singing.

I don't remember Momo ever correcting or scolding me for my little feelings of disappointment. She rode them out with me and was generally very cheerful and encouraging, ignoring my pout, continuing her happy spirit . . . listening to my concerns all the while.

Momo never met a stranger. She had her fingers in every pie. She'd plan a gathering, and somebody would tell her they couldn't come after all, because their brother's family had arrived unexpectedly with six kids and it would just be too much. "Absolutely not," Momo would laugh. "You pack up that family and bring 'em all over here for dinner. I'll add another bean to the pot." We often sat around the dinner table at Momo's with complete strangers and, on rare occasions, with other nationalities.

Momo . . . my wonderful grandmother

My mother also enjoyed entertaining. She set a beautiful table, was a wonderful cook, and knew how to make folks feel welcome—young or old, educated or uneducated, happy or sad.

Mother's thoughts were close to home, while Daddy thought far away. As I grew older and was in college, Mother's letters told of neighborhood happenings; Daddy's quoted Scripture and poetry. Mother mailed a new blouse or skirt, and Daddy sent books and my allowance. Both had their place. She kept my feet on the ground, and he helped me dream.

"You can be anything you want to be," Daddy would say to me. "You can go anywhere you want to go, achieve anything you like. You just have to line your desires up with the Lord's and go. You have to take a few risks and head out."

Once when I was really little and spending the night at a friend's house, I got very homesick at bedtime. I called Mother and Daddy and asked them to come get me. Immediately, Daddy got in the car and drove the few blocks to pick me up. I was embarrassed and told Daddy how sorry I was that I wasn't able to stay. I felt like a baby and asked him if he was mad at me because I called.

"Honey," he said, "of course I'm not mad at you. You can always call when you're afraid. I will always come get you if you need me to. But remember this—you are never alone wherever you are in life. God is with you. God will take care of you. Never be afraid to talk to God when you get homesick."

As we drove home that night, Daddy tucked into my heart a seed thought that has over time and travels grown into a giant tree, enabling me to go far and wide, high and low, across the world, virtually unafraid and excited about what lies down the road or over the horizon. And when I'm homesick, I talk to God about it.

Last year when I was landing in Europe, I whispered to myself, "First one to see Paris." Thank you, Daddy.

❦

During childhood I wish somebody had said to me these three loving words: "Please take notes." I often heard "I love you" or "I'm so sorry"—phrases most kids long to hear—but nobody ever said to me, "Write this down." And now that I'm looking back on those years and want to draw up information, it would be wonderful to have notes. If I were to encourage kids with a simple message with regard to their childhood, it would be to write stuff down, even the bad or difficult things. Once you grow up and your brain fills with reams of data, you really have to crane your brain to go back that far.

There are a couple of biggies, though, that I'll never forget about growing up in the Swindoll house. For one thing, my parents were very strong on "performing." By that I mean they wanted us to feel comfortable in front of people. (Certainly, they longed for us to behave, but that's another kind of performance.) To encourage this, Daddy often took us to Mr. Helmashack's Pharmacy. How old was I then—maybe six or seven? I don't know, but I remember being short, a little kid. The three of us were stairstep in height, so Daddy would line us up according to height on top of the counter, where we sang everything we knew. The prize for singing was dips of ice cream—the more verses, the more dips. A very cool reward!

Coupled with those little neighborhood performances, we also had frequent theater gatherings at Momo's house. Captive family members. Babe would quote poetry, Bubba would play piano, and I would act the fool. Literally. During those years, Danny Kaye was big in the movies, and he was my hero. I watched his performances then did my best to mimic him. The bigger the crowd, the more fun I had. Even though it was in a small living room, it might as well have been Carnegie Hall. *You've hit it big-time, Tutta.*

Oh, and Babe was absolutely fabulous at quoting poetry. We had between us a small book called *Poems Every Child Should Know* (red cover, frayed edges—I can see it in my mind's eye), which we often fought over, but somehow Babe got it more often than not. He memorized poems right and left and performed them to perfection during those evening soirées. I well remember the night he was quoting from memory Longfellow's poem "The Wreck of the *Hesperus*," and doing a fine job, I might add:

It was the schooner *Hesperus*,
    That sailed the wintry sea;
And the skipper had taken his little daughter,
    To bear him company.
Blue were her eyes as the fairy-flax,
    Her cheeks like the dawn of day,
And her bosom white as the hawthorn buds,
    That open the month of May.[1]

Tutta and Bubba
Two very happy kids... 1934

When Babe paused to take a breath, I whispered to Mother, "Babe said 'bosom.'" Mother sort of shrugged her shoulders and muttered something like, "Shhhh, just let him go on," looking at him approvingly and me disapprovingly.

Bubba's piano virtuosity was well known throughout the neighborhood. To me the sheet music looked like an undecipherable language, but to him it made perfect sense, and with the touch of his hands, he entertained us all. I remember my parents used to lay "grocery money" aside so Orville could take piano lessons from the best teacher in Houston. One night a week Mother drove him to his lesson, waited till he was finished, then drove home. To my knowledge they never missed—for years. We used to think he was going to be a famous concert pianist—because he kept telling us he was.

When I was about twelve, something interesting happened that impacted my thinking about the future. My folks gave me elocution lessons (probably to cure me of the Danny Kaye syndrome), and I absolutely loved that. Betty Green Little, a respected drama coach in Houston, taught the classes. She was probably the first person outside my own home who encouraged me to aim higher than the norm—the expected. Schoolteachers inadvertently conveyed that thought, of course, but this woman did it in a more personal way. Miss Little passed out sheets of paper that taught us proper pronunciation of words. We were given one sheet that had only the word "Oh" on it. She said, "When I call on you, please say 'oh' in the manner I tell you. Think before you speak how this 'oh' would sound, and then with all your heart, say it with that inflection."

I was in heaven.

"Lucille, please say 'oh' as though you're in pain."

I let out a cry as though I were dying. She smiled then said, "Now say 'oh' as if you were handed the baby to whom you had just given birth."

I let out the same cry. Miss Little laughed, as did the rest of the class.

On and on this exercise went with each of the five students saying "oh" in a dozen different ways: "Oh, how beautiful." "Oh, you can't mean it." "Oh no, not again."

Somewhere in the recesses of my mind that day I must have envisioned giving birth and disliked the idea. That guttural response to Miss Little's request was more than an answer to her question. It was a metaphor for things to come. Why? Who knows? It just seemed clear that getting married and having children—a most natural longing and certainly the course "expected" from girls of my generation—was simply not on my radar. *I don't want to follow the traditional path*, I thought. *I want to do life differently.* Can girls do something besides get married and have kids? In my twelve-year-old brain, I pondered that idea a lot. Of course, it was too early in my physical and emotional development to know exactly what I wanted in place of what most girls my age were aiming for. But I believe the seed thought Daddy had planted earlier began to grow heartily during those days: you are never alone . . . God is with you. Unwittingly, I had already left the dock on a unique journey the Lord had charted especially for me.

The second major positive thrust in my maturation process was an innate love for school. This I can't explain either. It was inside me. Neither of my parents had degrees of higher education, but both encouraged all three of us to enjoy school. I loved learning. Maybe I would have enjoyed it just as much apart from their prompting, but to have them cheer me on made an indelible impact, I'm sure. I wasn't a crackerjack student. I studied hard and applied myself but often came up with average grades, while both brothers were always on the honor roll. I had a lot of fun though, and that was more important in my way of thinking. Learn something new while having a good time—this was my mantra. *If I can do this all my life*, I thought, *I've got it made.*

What turned my crank most was figuring out how things work—gadgets, the world, my mind, problems, ideas—I spent a lot of time thinking about what I read or drew, investigated or discovered. Why didn't somebody write that wonderful book by David Macaulay, *The Way Things Work*, during my childhood? I would have memorized every word. I own three copies now. Friends who know me well have given them to me.

Taking Daddy at his word made me think I could accomplish anything, so I tried it all. I built model airplanes and boats, played cello, swam in competition, dissected frogs, made up games, took calculus. (Got a rotten grade in that last one, but at least I tried.)

Going to the library was like a holiday. I checked out books about other countries, art, music, and anything that had to do with building things. I decorated my little bedroom bulletin board with notes from friends, letters from Momo, simple drawings, and magazine cutouts of faraway places with strange sounding names that I dreamed of seeing one day. When I sat at my desk at night doing homework, I imagined myself in another world, another time or place. I was an inventor. Explorer. Naturalist. Musician. Artist. Anthropologist. Singer. On and on. Interestingly, none of these visualizations ever included the white picket fence, the husband, three kids, and a dog. I saw myself as free to roam the world without any attachments, meeting people from everywhere.

There is much about me that is not transferable to anybody else. That's true of everyone, of course. But as I write this today, I see again how God had his hand on my future from the very beginning. For the life of me I can't tell you what primary ingredient made me who I am. And surely there isn't only one. If there is, I can't separate it out from everything else. The only thing I can do is say for a fact that God creates each of us uniquely by his design and for his purpose. He readies the path that beckons us in the direction he has in mind. And when we step onto the path, the adventure begins.

☆ "FAR AWAY" - Some more travel - the NorthEast U.S.;
Banff + Vancouver. China? Paris?
Quebec. Lots of RV travels in the U.S.

"Mother's thoughts were close to home, while Daddy thought far away. She kept my feet on the ground, and he helped me dream." When you think of "close to home," what comes to mind? When you think of "far away," what do you dream of and hope for?

7/23/10 Home = Houston, TX. More precisely home is 19727 Sage Tree Trail, Humble TX. This home Tim + I have lived in for 6-7 yrs. Ben never lived @ this house.

Home where Ben's concerned would be New Orleans (the best, friendliest neighborhood we lived in) OR 3307 Falling Brook - Kingwood. Good memories @ this address, but also some bad, sad ones. We lived there for 20 years. We had problems w/ Ben there. I also think back to alot of years that I suffered from depression there.

☆ "Far Away"? My 1st thought was Terlingua - hope for a long + happy retirement w/ Tim. My biggest hope? That Tim would accept Christ as Savior.

I liked what Lucy said on p. 7 " you just have to line your desires up w/ the Lord's + go. Lord, I so desire to do Your will. To be used by you to show people around me your love.

Tim & I just returned from a 2-wk trip to Italy. (June 18-July 4, 2010). Very interesting & very nice to have 2 weeks w/ Tim.

Today — an ordinary day — worked out w/ Dana; a few chores @ home; lunch w/ Sharon James; shopping @ the mall. I have recently lost 20 actual # (25# body fat). I have been having a ball buying new, cute clothes. I just got 3 really cute tops, a purse & shoes — all on sale!!! — for my trip to Minnesota for Jessica's wedding. Thank you Lord for all of the blessings you've given me. You are so incredibly good to me. I know I don't have to earn this, but I do want to make you proud!

Like Lucy, I want to remember that I'm never alone & that I can always turn to you Lord when I'm homesick.

The world is an enormous place.

Mark the places on this map you'd like to visit and write about why.

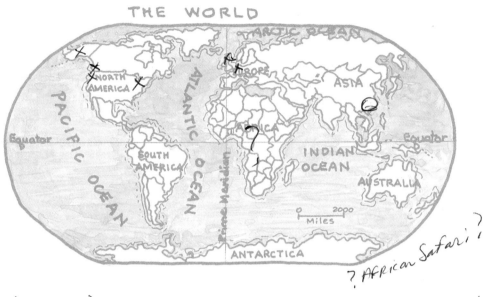

? African Safari?

x Alaska ⎫ breath-taking beauty.
x Canada ⎬ very different from what I'm used to.
I want to see polar bears + grizzly bears + ice bergs +
whales.
x N E America — Also different culture, pretty leaves + sea shore
China — wow! very foreign. Shari Woods is
organizing a trip for Fall 2011 — 22 days. I'm
not sure I'd want to go for that long of + Soyful would
be difficult — but not impossible.
Paris — Versailles + the Louvre
Scotland — green hills — more beauty.
Lord, you've given me a love for your creation.
I love being outside + seeing new things
that you've made.

7/23/10

What happened today? My loving Father God
Knew exactly what I needed & has provided
it to me.

I'm struggling w/ binge-eating again + also
with motivation to exercise + do this. (I'm
worried it's being off Cymbalta - 2 months now).

Anyway - I told my personal trainer Dana
about this + she said to write my
"Mission Statement" this weekend.

What do I want for my life?
How will "getting healthy" affect me?
What will it change for me?

I stopped in Barnes + Noble to say hi
to Melissa Arlt and saw this book.
Lord, thank you for leading me to this.
This is helping me w/ my Mission Statement.
This book is your gift to me - yet another
beautiful gift from my loving Father.
Thank you Lord.

(If I wasn't sitting in the mall, I'd
sing "I love you Lord + I lift my voice...
but even I'm not that crazy!

P. 19 "Nothing goes to waste in God's
                              economy."

Being reared in a home like mine had its challenges. While we were a loving, patriotic, upstanding, Christian family, there were patterns and mores that governed the thinking of my parents (especially Mother), and one didn't deviate from those without unpleasant consequences. It was 1950 when I graduated from high school and time for me to consider college, then of course, marriage. Many of my friends skipped the college part, got engaged and married right off the bat.

I talked to my dad about wanting to go to college and some of my dreams for the future, which still didn't include a wedding. He was very supportive, and I felt that support, but it was hard to escape the overriding petulant moods of my mother when I mentioned these things to her. Because I was young and had no autonomy, and because peer pressure was rampant among church and school friends, as well as from Mother, I began dating a Christian boy who was sort of the "catch" of our group . . . very handsome and kind. Eventually we began "going steady," and I was given an engagement ring the summer before college began. These were confusing months for me because my heart was torn. I didn't love this young man the way one should when marriage is in the offing, but I so wanted to please Mother that I accepted the ring and went away to college, engaged and insecure.

After a few months on campus, it was obvious to me that the world was an enormous place, my dreams were very different from "settling down," as Mother used to say, and this engagement had to be called off.

I went home for a weekend, told the boy I was not the one for him, returned the ring, and apparently broke his heart and (more importantly) my mom's. Once again, Daddy came to my rescue, but Mother's disappointment with me was apparent for a very long time. The boy recovered; it seemed Mother never would!

During these tumultuous months, an important principle began to build inside me: No matter what, you have to be yourself. These minuscule threads of thought started roping together over time to become the fiber of my person. I learned it was okay to be myself and like myself—and survive—in spite of my mother's strong disapproval. She had no category for me because I thwarted her domestic dreams for her only daughter. What was to become of me if I ended up without a husband?

Please understand, I'm not opposed to marriage. I believe it to be a God-given, sacred institution, one that is blessed and encouraged by Scripture. I just wasn't compelled to make it part of my personal journey. And in the fifties, I can tell you, not to marry was deeply criticized by the general Christian community. I was the first person in my extended family who chose to remain single. It was a hard row to hoe, and I've often wondered where I would be now had it not been for the allegiance and love of my father. If he ever in his heart preferred marriage for me, I never knew it, and he never criticized me for choosing the path I did. Would that every girl had a dad like mine.

In retrospect, there were two teachers who also quietly (but deeply) influenced me to be myself. One in high school, the other in college. The first was a man, the second a woman, both in the field of music.

Eugene Seastrand taught in Houston's Milby High School and was truly a genius. Mr. Seastrand played every instrument, led the glee club, was tenderhearted and very attentive to his students. He always encouraged us to do more, reach higher, try new things, and dream big. As a teenager, I placed him among my heroes. (He did everything left-handed. That fascinated me. He'd pick up the ukulele, stroke the strings with his left hand, and actually make music. All the chords were backward, but it seemed to work. When I tried playing my ukulele that way, it was cacophony.)

Mr. Seastrand encouraged me to learn to play the cello. Oh my! I loved the sonorous tones of a cello, but it never occurred to me I could tackle such an instrument. "You can play anything you want to, Lucille," Mr. Seastrand would say. "Don't limit yourself to only one instrument or only one thing. It takes a lot of practice to do things well, but everybody should have a beginning knowledge of all the instruments. Why don't you try the cello?" And so I did.

During these days, Orville was continuing his wizardry on the piano, and Chuck was playing clarinet, saxophone, bassoon, and flute—all due to the influence and loving motivation of Mr. Seastrand. I was in the glee club, learning to sight-read music, and enjoying every minute of it. These classes took my mind off the turmoil with Mother, and they set patterns that added to the stepping-stones toward individuation and independence. It never occurred to me that God was at work in my life—I was too busy living it—but he was using everything to help me grow up to be the unique person he tenderly and expertly created me to be. Nothing goes to waste in God's economy.

By the time I graduated from high school, I had developed such a love for music that I seriously considered pursuing a musical career and even majored in voice my first year in college. The first teacher I met at Mary Hardin-Baylor College in Belton, Texas, was Florence Bergendahl. She was my faculty adviser. Now, there was one formidable woman! She was right out of a Wagner opera, and you don't fool with those Wagnerian sopranos, let me tell you.

"Bergie" was head of the vocal department, and everything about her fascinated me. She was tall, with a majestic presence, perfect posture, purposeful stride, and a booming voice. "So you want to sing, Lucille. You want to be a soloist?"

"Yes, ma'am."

"We'll see about that. Generally people do what they want to in life if they want it bad enough. In time, we'll see how bad you want it."

"Yes, ma'am."

I was terrified and spellbound. Bergie challenged my thinking on every front. What was I reading? Why did I believe that? Where did I want to live, given a choice? Did I want to see the world? What were my aspirations? How badly did I want to sing? Was I thinking original thoughts? How far did I want to go in life? What were the enemies of my soul? On and on and on. I spent hours talking with Miss Bergendahl, and every time I did, I expanded inside.

I was singing in Italian, French, and German, but to pronounce the words correctly wasn't good enough for Bergie. What did they mean? Why did I think the librettist chose that word instead of another? Why were those specific dynamics or nuances used at that moment, with that word? Questions, all the time. And Bergie wanted answers! I had to think. She wanted me to know the value of researching music—and life.

By the second semester, I had become Miss Bergendahl's most devoted student and admirer. Everything she did and was, I wanted to do and be. On one occasion she invited me to her home, and then I was really hooked. The walls were covered with paintings and memorabilia she had collected on her travels abroad. There were awards and trophies, framed drawings of famous composers, and countless opera scores on her bookshelves. She told me how she loved reading the *New York Times* every day, and that she sang along with all the Metropolitan opera performers on the Saturday afternoon radio programs.

She even confessed to me the private anguish of her soul when the man she loved was killed in an automobile accident and her hopes and dreams for a life with him were shattered. She recounted the time she discovered a lump in her breast, which turned out to be malignant, resulting in a radical mastectomy. She was living alone at the time and had very little money to pay for the surgery. "How did you manage?" I asked.

"Well, you just trust God with your life, child. You call the hospital, set up a room for yourself, tell the doctor you hope he knows what he's doing, and go have the surgery. After all, if your faith doesn't work when the chips are down, and you never use it . . . what good is it anyway?"

Bergie had little homilies by which she lived. Things like, "Straighten up. Never slouch. A good soloist stands tall and gets down to business." And, "Give yourself to the music . . . don't hold back. Think. Think." And, "Your voice is you. It reflects who you are inside—your joys, sorrows, gains, losses, fullness, emptiness. Your voice is the vehicle that people know as you. Use it wisely."

Florence Bergendahl, my brilliant, formidable voice teacher

My favorite saying of Bergie's was, "Look alive! Nobody wants to watch a dead person sing. Smile. Sing out!"

For some reason, I thought majoring in voice meant standing up and singing. Period. I could do that. But what I couldn't do was comprehend the ingredients of music. That wasn't singing; that was work! The desire to major in voice flew out the window once I got into a music theory class. Suddenly I was having to learn about metric units, rhythmic patterns, tempos, metronomic cadences—all the definitions and quasi-mathematical formulas that go into music's foundation. Instead of being fun, studying music became tedious and hard.

So, as most college students do at least once, I changed my major. I chose commercial art for a couple of reasons. First, I had always loved art; it ran in my family's veins. My mother's sister (Aunt Ernestine) was a wonderful artist, and she and I often talked about painting and drawing. She'd encourage me to make little drawings of what I was doing or what I saw. My dad was a cartoonist. He was pretty good, too. Not great, but good enough to be a source of inspiration for me.

Second, like many students, I was looking for an easy path toward a career, and since the field of art didn't seem as difficult to get my arms around as music, I thought, *Well, if I can't make music into what I want it to be, maybe I can be an artist.* Little did I realize that I would end up using everything I learned, everywhere I worked, for as long as I lived. Every class I took, every experience I had in both school and life, ultimately was woven together by the Master Artist into the person I've become—a sort of jack-of-all trades but master of none!

While majoring in art, I continued to study voice and ultimately gave a senior recital. On the night of that voice recital in 1955, just prior to graduation, Miss Bergendahl gave me a lovely present—two books from her personal library: *An Anthology* by Albert Schweitzer and *An Autobiography* by Frank Lloyd Wright. In her travels, Bergie had the opportunity to meet both of these men, and the latter book was autographed to her by the famous architect himself. I still have them, of course, and they're among my treasures. When she handed me the books, Bergie said, "This gift is to express my love for you, Lucille. You've come a long way, and I'm proud of your accomplishments. You sang a beautiful recital tonight. You got down to business!"

Ten years later I saw Florence Bergendahl for the last time. I had been invited to sing at the school's Charter Day homecoming festivities, and she was there. We had a sweet reunion, talking of many things—her life, my life, the world, music, travel, the times in which we lived. About a week later, in the mail came a note from my teacher and friend. It read:

> *Your voice is beautiful, my dear—more resonant and richer in quality. The Saturday morning solo was a delight—everyone listened with genuine pleasure. I watched their faces.*

Miss Bergendahl is dead now and has been for many years. She went to her grave never knowing how deeply she influenced the course of my life. Her influence reaches far and wide even today. When I stand on stages around the country, speaking to large audiences, I often think of her. In the back of my mind, I can hear her words: Stand tall. Get down to business. Your voice is you.

After graduating from college, I reluctantly moved back home, dreading impending encounters with Mother. But I immediately noticed an amazing, favorable change in her. She didn't rail on me or try to persuade me to change my life. She left me alone; not only that, but she encouraged me to be myself. This was unheard of. Mother stopped trying to force me to think anything apart from what seemed right to me. She stopped telling me what to do or how to dress or that my views were too far-fetched. She did, in fact, encourage me to live exactly as I wanted to. In short, she let me be free. It was a wonderful feeling, to say the least, and because of that kindness I drew closer to Mother. This was a miracle in our household, and was a result, I soon learned, of their attendance at a church that had an outstanding Bible teacher as the pastor.

Having accepted the Lord as a preteen, I was acquainted with the basic conditions of salvation but knew little about doctrine and the magnificent treasures to be mined by studying God's Word. I was a greenhorn, as were my folks. For years we had attended a church that taught little more than that there was a rule for everything, defensible by Scripture. We were steeped in legalism. We knew little to nothing of the grace of God, freedom in Christ, and theology that endorsed individuality and liberty. In my circle of relationships, everybody told everybody else how to live, what to think, and where to enlist. I hated that, and I especially hated it from my mother. I longed for the freedom to investigate things on my own without being constantly criticized for going "off the beaten track."

My parents told me the pastor at their new church had graduated magna cum laude from Dallas Theological Seminary and was a lieutenant colonel in the Air Force reserves and a former Rhodes scholar. They invited me to go hear him one night, and out of curiosity I accepted. His academic credentials alone appealed to me, and I found everything my parents had said to be true. This man did indeed know God's Word and taught it in a formal, comprehensible, delineating way that I found very attractive. It was a left-brained approach without a lot of emotion or hype. Just facts and truth and credible, practical information.

As I began to have this magnificent Book opened to me in such a palatable way, I absolutely fell in love with Jesus Christ. Everything about his deity and humanity held my interest. Mother, Daddy, and I went to those classes four nights a week and every Sunday for a period of two years, and it would have taken an act of Congress for me to do otherwise. I lived for those classes, took copious notes, and studied my Bible all the time; and they were almost all I talked about with my parents. It may sound terribly one-tracked, and it was I'm sure, but I was the sponge that drank the ocean. I could not get enough. I went in dying of thirst and found the fountain of life.

I began memorizing Scripture and learning about all the promises and blessings that were mine by virtue of simply putting my faith in Christ. They were there all along, but no one had ever taught them to me. Not only did thee, after the pattern of the ¹tabernacle, and the pattern of all the instruments thereof, even so shall ye make *it*.

The tabernacle: (1) the ark.

10 And they shall ᵃmake an ²ark of ³shittim wood: two cubits and a half *shall be* the length thereof, and a cubit and a half the breadth thereof, and a cubit and a half the height thereof.

11 And thou shalt overlay it with pure gold, within and without shalt thou overlay it, and shalt make upon it a crown of gold round about.

12 And thou shalt cast four rings of gold for it, and put *them* in the four corners thereof; and two rings *shall be* in the one side of it, and two rings in the other side of it.

13 And thou shalt make staves *of* shittim wood, and overlay them with gold.

B.C. 1491

ᵃ The most inclusive

Gr.
Christ.
Gold =
Deity; wood

"THE TABERNACLE"

seat shall ye make the cherubims on the two ends thereof.

20 And the cherubims shall stretch forth *their* wings on high, covering the mercy seat with their wings, and their faces *shall look* one to another; toward the mercy seat shall the faces of the cherubims be.

21 And thou shalt put the mercy seat above upon the ark; and in the ark thou shalt put the testimony that I shall give thee.

22 And there I will meet with thee, and I will commune with thee from above the mercy seat, from between the two cherubims which are upon the ark of the testimony

"THE HOLY OF HOLIES"
(THE VERY PRESENT GOD.)

...ways: (1) of the Church as a habitation of the Spirit (Eph. 2. 19-22); (2) of the believer (2 Cor. 6. 16); (3) of the Father of things in the heavens (Heb. 9. 23, 24). In *detail*, all speaks of Christ: (1) the ark, in its materials, acacia-wood (see Ex. 26. 15, *note*) and gold, is a type of the humanity and deity of Christ. (2) In its *contents*, a type of Christ, as: (a) having God's law in His heart (Ex. 25. 16); (b) the wilderness food (or portion) of His people (Ex. 16. 33); (c) Himself the resurrection, of which Aaron's rod is the symbol (Num. 17. 10). (3) In its use the ark, especially the mercy-seat, was a type of God's throne. That it was, to the believer, a throne of grace and not of judgment, was due to the mercy-seat, of gold and sprinkled with the blood of atonement, which vindicated the law and the divine holiness guarded by the cherubim (Gen. 3. 24; Mk. 1. 5, note). See *Propitiation*, Rom. 3. 25, *note*.

All begins with the ark, which, in the completed tabernacle, was placed in the holy of holies, because, in *revelation*, God begins from Himself, working outward toward man; as, in *approach*, the worshipper begins from himself, moving toward God in the holy of holies. The same order is seen in the Levitical offerings (Lev. 1-5). In *approach* man begins at the brazen altar, type of the Cross, where, in the fire of judgment, atonement is made.

"ARK, MERCY, and CHERUBIM"
(Propitiation, Rom.) ⑨

⑩

"BRAZEN LAVER"
(Cleansing, 1 John 1: 9)

⑶

"BRAZEN ALTAR"
(The Cross) ⑵

"GATE"
(Christ The Way, John 14: 6) ⑴

this time commitment benefit me in terms of a personal, strong doctrinal foundation regarding my faith but also through those days, weeks, and months my mother and I addressed the differences that had crippled our relationship for years. Once that happened, the breach between us was healed, and we remained close until the day Mother died in 1971.

What is it about the Bible that catches us off guard? That reaches into the depths of our souls and little by little begins to straighten us out? It digs up our arrogance and pride and enables us to forgive and forget. It creates spaces for understanding that we would not have thought possible, much less tolerated. Nothing of humankind can do that for us. Only God's Spirit has the ability to reach that deep into a life. The Word of God is powerful enough to change darkness to light and dissatisfaction to joy. I truly believe that, and what happened between Mother and me is the proof. Neither of us had the capacity to change ourselves, but the supernatural work of the Holy Spirit did.

This is a fairly typical photo of mother & dad. They loved to dress up... probably going to church.

All the money in the world could not buy what I now have inside. Those two years of attending Bible classes night after night after night truly set in place my credo and gave me the spiritual training I needed to face things on my own. I'm not implying I don't need people, because I certainly do; but I am saying that once God's incorruptible truth became the protoplasm of my soul, I knew without doubt that he would make a way for me to be truly myself—apart from having anybody else in my life—growing in him and sensing his presence when I relied on what he said. He was even better than my father, whom I adored—and that is saying a lot. My relationship with Jesus Christ provided both eternal life and abundant life, and I took him at his word on both counts.

What was I going to do now—out of college with all this newfound spiritual thrust pushing me forward? The job market loomed before this twenty-three-year-old, and it was my oyster. In the exuberance of my youth, I considered many things. I even thought it might be a kick to be a bartender. Really. Think about it. Tending bar had everything I liked: I could learn something new while having a good time. Make things with my hands. It was absolutely devoid of legalism. And I didn't have to be married. A shoo-in. I could dispense little tidbits of wit and wisdom while serving drinks and get paid for it. Didn't have to get into deep counseling (which I didn't want to do), but I could listen to the problems of others, crack a few jokes, and send them on their way jollier folks.

The second occupation I considered was being a telephone repairman. The young man to whom I had been engaged was one, and he was a crackerjack. Every day he climbed poles, looked down on the rest of the world, listened in on other people's private conversations, and told me how much fun it was. And best of all, when you repaired telephone lines, you got to wear one of those adorable little leather pouches at the waist that held your tools. I gravitated to that big-time. I've always loved tools and having them at the ready. Right there would be a hammer, screwdriver, knife, wrench, fuse puller, wire stripper, pliers, and droplight. The works.

As a little girl, my dad had actually taught me how to use tools properly and take care of them. He'd given me my first toolbox (a tiny container that held smaller versions of his tools), and together we repaired appliances around the house: lamps, radios, clocks, fences, lawn mowers, and our pièce de résistance—the toilet. So, to have a job that enabled me to use tools captivated my interest.

I never pursued either of these occupations, but I'm still enthralled. What I think would really be neat is being a bartender who wears a pouch with swizzle sticks, whisk, bottle opener, spatula, whistle, and small New Testament. With the whistle I could call the cops when need be, and a New Testament would come in handy for looking up forgotten verses when helping somebody.

The Lord had a slightly different plan in mind, but the early injunction from my dad—you can be anything you want to be, do anything you want to do—kept me constantly curious about what that might mean. I was ready, set to go. And the adventure continued . . .

Negotiate. Laugh at yourself. Quit taking life so seriously.
Stop personalizing everything that comes your way. You'll live longer.

_____

_____

_____

_____

_____

_____

_____

_____

_____

_____

_____

_____

_____

_____

_____

_____

_____

_____

three years, sans furlough, with the

Things of value cannot be had for nothing.

What do you value most?

What is the "price" of being true to your own values?

Everything starts simply—simple lines, simple thoughts, simple premises.
How would you like to simplify your life? What will you do to get started?

Life has no shortcuts.

The first time I ever left home on my own I was sixteen. Went by train from Houston to Fort Worth to visit cousins. I'll never forget that day. My daddy took a picture of me in my good blue dress Mother had made, my Sunday shoes, and a matching purse. I wore a cute little hat and carried white gloves. *Watch out, world. Here I come!* I was so excited I could hardly breathe—a bit scared because I'd never been anywhere by myself, but jazzed at the idea of taking a trip.

The feeling I had that day has never left. Every year since then I've taken a trip, maybe not a long one, but something that involved packing a bag and spending the night. And more often than not, I've made numerous trips each year.

There has always been something in me that wanted to go! And it's not just my nature; it's compatible with my faith. While inhabiting the earth in bodily form, Jesus had a lot to say about going. He was forever sending someone somewhere on a mission. He commanded his disciples to follow, wherever he happened to be going. And his last word of instruction to us, his followers, before returning to his heavenly Father was "Go" (Matthew 28). Jesus is interested in our looking beyond ourselves, taking the next step, reaching out, and going.

It's kind of strange that I want to go so much, because I'm truly a homebody. I love owning a home and thoroughly enjoy being in it. I like to keep house and figure things out around the place. I love to cook and entertain and decorate. But none of that squelches my desire to wander around the world in search of adventure. It's as if that wanderlust was put in me as part of my genetic makeup, and it becomes more of a passion the older I get.

Even when I'm not on the road physically, my heart reaches out to the world. I read about people who live everywhere and have been everywhere. I care what happens to them and how they live. I want to know more—to understand their ways, their culture, their history, and their perspectives. I believe it's a mission that God himself has put in all of us. As believers, we do not live on an island. We are part of a great universe of people who are loved by God, and his desire is that, as his children, we care about others.

Before the Lord takes me home, I want to go everywhere—meet new people, visit museums, hear music, see architecture, sample different foods (well, maybe not all foods)—generally speaking, I want to check out everything for myself. Will I live long enough to make this dream come true? Who knows? But I do know if I don't dream it and think about it and plan it, I'll never go anywhere. In Bergie's words, "Generally people do what they want to in life if they want it bad enough. In time, we'll see how bad you want it."

Adventure starts in the mind then travels to the heart. If it lodges there long enough, it heads to the ticket counter, gets on the plane, and flies to China. I've never been to China.

I haven't always had the privilege of being a road warrior. The desire to go was in me, but I lacked opportunity and resources. Ready for a giant risk two years out of college, I moved from Houston to Dallas in 1957. Having a degree in commercial art helped me land a job with Mobil Oil Corporation as a draftsman. I thought I'd be there a couple years then go back to school because I loved school and everything that went with it. But as I got more into corporate life, I discovered some advantages that seemed more valuable to me. I found I could make a good living, continually learn new and interesting things, feel secure in a job while pursuing all kinds of other interests outside the office, enjoy an esprit de corps at work, and develop a professional life—something I had never experienced before. I didn't know these things for a fact then, but everything I was doing rang true in my spirit. It felt right. It was a lot like school, only better.

It wasn't always easy, of course. There were days I wanted to throw in the towel—one that was soaking wet with the tears of disappointment over something that didn't go my way or over hard work without recognition, but I hung in there. Ultimately it paid off, both emotionally and financially.

Almost before I knew it, I had been at Mobil thirty years! I was busy living life, not standing around counting the years nor bemoaning the fact that I had to report to work every day instead of going to places I longed to see. By the time I retired in 1987, I was the manager of the Rights of Ways and Claims department, handling negotiations, contracts, real-estate problems, easements, a sizable budget, and a small staff of employees. And fortunately I had saved enough money to have a nice nest egg that could be rolled over into a retirement fund. Everything Daddy had taught me came into play.

One of the greatest lessons I tucked under my belt during this time was this: things of value cannot be had for nothing. My years at Mobil Oil Corporation were the testing ground for this truth. More often than not, deferring the rewards of today gives us the future we dream of tomorrow. We have to spend in order to get—and time, energy, and money are our only mediums of exchange. Count on it, anticipate it, and accept it. When we get this straight and realize there's no shortcut to having what we want, life gets a bit easier. Not problem-free, but definitely easier. We're not nearly as frustrated because we settle into the patterns that pay off in our souls and bodies. We quit thinking that life somehow owes us a living. We work. We pray. We study. We're attentive to details. We put first things first. We risk. We believe God means what he says. Unless we live out of these truths, there really is no tomorrow. Everything becomes one endless, tedious, tiresome "today," and there's no growth or change. In short, wisdom never comes.

I remember asking God for wisdom. It was as though he asked me one day when I was praying, "What do you want most, Luci?" I started thinking about where I had been and some of the choices I'd made that led to dead ends. After turning all this over in my mind, I answered, "Wisdom, Lord." That's what I want most. Please, give me wisdom.

Well, when we ask for that all kinds of things begin to happen. Things we hadn't planned on. God comes in like a flood, altering our world—changing the things we once valued, restructuring relationships, taking away this desire and adding that one, putting our priorities in a new alignment. God grows us up! Sara Teasdale wrote a poem about this very thing, called "Wisdom."

When I have ceased to break my wings
Against the faultiness of things,
And learned that compromises wait
Behind each hardly opened gate,
When I can look Life in the eyes,
Grown calm and very coldly wise,
Life will have given me the Truth,
And taken in exchange—my youth.[2]

When life began giving me the truth, I often felt loss or uncertainty. At times I was adrift without moorings. I experienced fear and redirection, or no direction. I felt afraid. Amazing as it seems, though, I rarely felt alone; certainly lonely at times, but always tethered to God in some indefinable way. I knew God was with me and for me. I often didn't have a clue about his inscrutable ways of handling things (and I still don't), but deep inside there was an abiding assurance that he would keep his word and, somehow, bring me out on the other side.

In college I memorized a poem that came to mind on many occasions during those years with Mobil: "The Hound of Heaven" by English poet Francis Thompson. In these closing lines God is addressing his child, hounding him so to speak, as he pursues him in the highways and byways of life. Reviewing these words helped me continue to believe God truly cared about me and that my dependence on him was well placed. These words helped me remember that God never meant me harm or loneliness or fear. He simply wanted me to find what I needed in him.

I'm in costume for the Opera, ANNA BOLENA

All which I took from thee, I did but take not for thy harms,
But just that thou mightst seek it in My arms.
All which thy child's mistake fancies as lost, I have stored
  for thee at home:
Rise, clasp My hand and come![3]

God gave me the wisdom to pursue other interests while I worked eight to five during the week. In fact, during those years characterized by constant routine, I found a joyful outlet for my soul. Answering a tiny newspaper ad in the *Dallas Morning News* about chorus auditions, I was accepted for the 1959 season with the Dallas Civic Opera Company. For fifteen years, from 1959 to 1973, I sang my heart out. It didn't come without sacrifice and tons of expended energy, but it gave me one of the greatest experiences of my life. It was an exciting, enjoyable adventure, and the funny thing is, it could not have come at a better time. I know now it would have been unattainable at any other point in my life, and if I'd waited, I would have missed it. I absolutely couldn't do it today—when no two days are ever the same and my lifestyle takes me in a hundred different directions. This unusual opportunity for great adventure was placed in my path at a juncture when my daily routine was lived stereotypically.

I worked each day at Mobil and in the evenings either rehearsed for performances or sang in the productions. The experience introduced me to fascinating people from all over the world, and it enlarged my boundaries in a way nothing else could. Even though everything was brand-new to me, I entered in with abandonment and joy. With every new person I met, every new performance, I was renewed. It was wonderful!

Opera is a strange phenomenon to many people. As someone remarked to me, "It's educated screeching"—an indictment I can understand when one knows nothing about the music. But to those of us who love it, it can become a time-consuming passion. Opera engages every one of the arts:

painting, dance, singing, orchestration, costumes—the works! Everything that makes up live theater is only enhanced on the operatic stage.

While living in Houston years before, I'd attended my first opera, *Carmen*. Had a seat on the front row. Such beautiful music! Dimitri Mitropoulus lifted his baton to begin conducting the overture, and I thought I'd faint. I was enraptured for the next two hours. It's an unforgettable memory. So, to have been an active part of an opera company was terribly exciting.

The year I stopped singing in the Dallas chorus I painted a small plaque that lists all thirty-four operas in which I sang. My favorite, *Lucia di Lammermoor* by Donizetti, is the first on the list. The plaque hangs in my library, at the end of a bookcase that holds opera books, music scores, and old performance programs. There are lots of memories in that room. I turn the corner out of my studio and—*bam!*—I'm transported back thirty-eight years. I thank God I had such a unique, life-changing experience that so broadened my world and my understanding of it. And here's what's amazing—during those busy years I hardly ever left town!

LUCIA DI LAMMERMOOR · LA BOHEME
MEDEA · DAUGHTER OF THE REGIMENT
DON GIOVANNI · SAMSON ET DALILA
MADAMA BUTTERFLY · LA TRAVIATA
ALCINA · PAGLIACCI · ANNA BOLENA
UN BALLO IN MASCHERA · MESSIAH
THAIS · OTELLO · DIDO AND AENEAS
SUOR ANGELICA · ANDREA CHENIER
CORONATION OF POPPEA · MACBETH
JULIUS CAESAR · CARMEN · FIDELIO
AIDA · ORPHEUS IN THE UNDERWORLD
FAERIE QUEEN · NOZZE DI FIGARO
CARMINA BURANA · FEDORA · TOSCA
MERRY WIDOW · COQ D'OR · LA FAVORITA

Except . . . the time opera friends who lived in Europe invited me to visit. Taking them at their word, I took my first trip to Europe in 1966. While there I visited La Scala, in Milan, Italy. Norberto Mola, chorus master of the La Scala Opera Chorus for over forty years, had been with us in Dallas for a three-month season after his retirement. Now back in Milan, he saw to it that I got a tour of the local opera house and a box seat right square in the center of the balcony. There I was, the El Campo Kid, watching a performance in the world's most famous opera house, like I was somebody! First one to see La Scala.

To take that first trip to Europe, I saved twenty-five dollars a month for five years, and when I landed on foreign soil, there wasn't a day when my feet touched the ground. I walked on air, elated over everything—the countries, cities, people, art, music, food, languages, flights, and accommodations. I had discovered a new world and knew then I'd never get my fill. That twenty-one-day trip opened a whole universe of wonder—a zoom lens into endless possibilities. It whetted an appetite that has never been satiated. The travel itself (not to mention the destinations) keeps me going back for more.

Shortly after I got home from that first trip to Europe, I bought a world globe. Nothing expensive or fancy, just a round ball on a stand that I could twirl and watch the countries go by. Every place I saw or touched, I wanted to experience for myself. I wanted to go there.

I have a big, elaborate world globe now. It has all the longitude and latitude lines and clearly marked topography, and every day I fool with that thing. Sometimes I just twirl it and think about the cultures spinning across my mind's eye. Sometimes I look up a place in my atlas then find it on the globe. When something earth shattering happens on the other side of the world, and I read about it in the newspaper or see it happen on TV, I go over to the globe and find that very spot. If I'm reading a book that talks about a particular place in the ocean or on a mountain peak, I check it out on my world. I like knowing what country borders on another, where the oceans meet, what's on the equator. I'm a nut for all that stuff.

Even though the world is huge, there's something personal and intimate about it when we can get our arms around it. When the earth is in front of

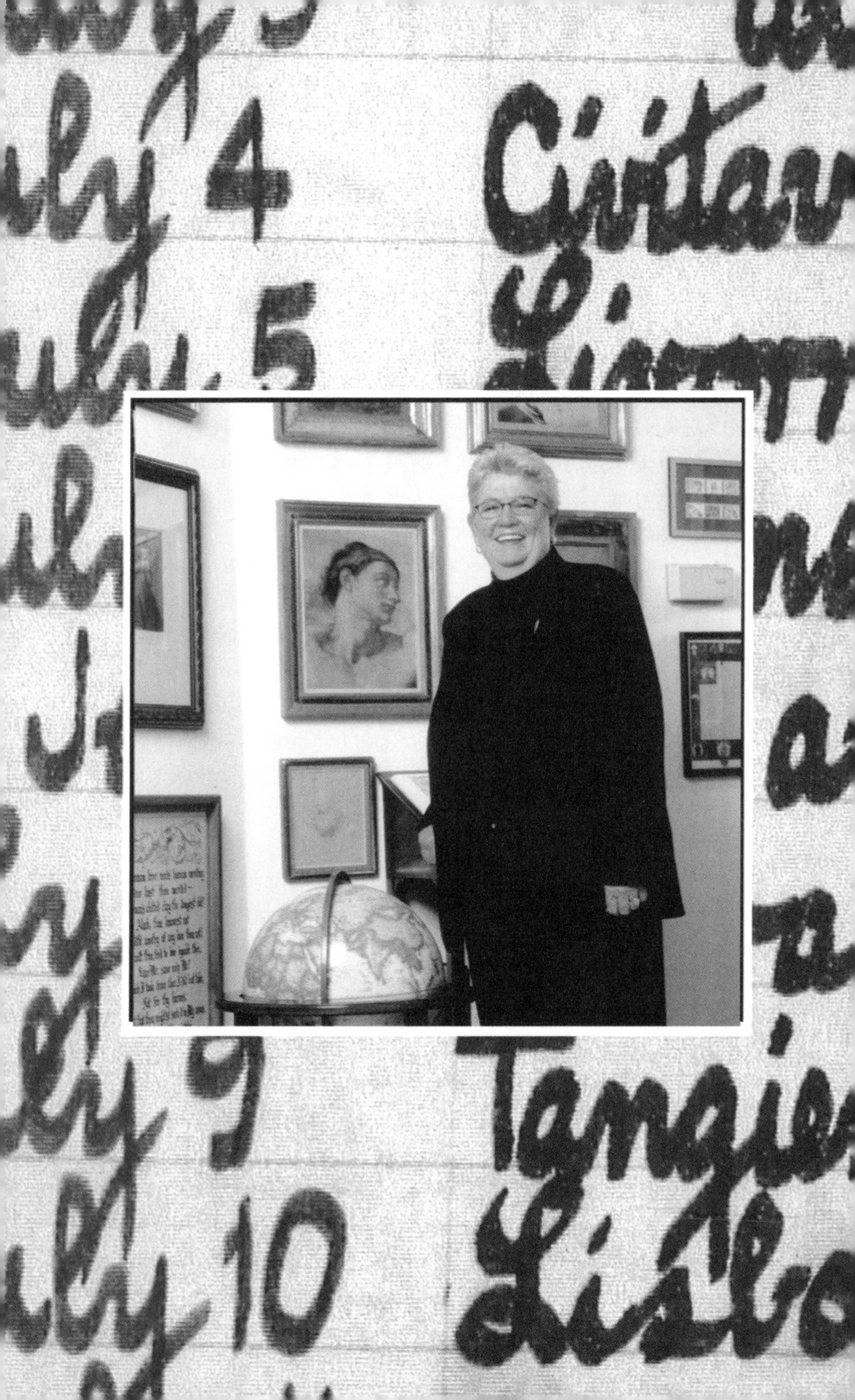

us, in a round ball, with all the countries and oceans delineated, it makes everything seem accessible, within reach. No borders or boundaries or impasses. I love that. Problems that exist in actuality between nations and continents can't be seen on a world globe or map, and everything is peaceful. Anything is possible. Every act of kindness or desire for betterment seems doable.

This kind of outlook gives us the capacity to dream big, dare to try new things, and believe we can overcome detours and obstacles that get in our way or hold us back. If the world isn't such an ominous, scary place, then we are more inclined to reach out to others and give our hearts to them.

I want to give my heart to others.

❧

Seventeen years ago a very dear friend of mine died from the ravages of cancer, a disease she fought valiantly for seventeen years but finally lost. Her name was Joanne DeGraw. Joanne and I shared the same Texas roots, philosophy of life, faith in Jesus Christ, sense of humor, and love for all things beautiful. She was an interior decorator, a world traveler, the wife of an attorney, mother of two grown children, and grandmother to one.

I had visited Joanne in her home in Northern California, and she had been the decorator for my home in Southern California. We've sat long hours over a meal or in front of a fireplace laughing, telling stories, discussing books, theater, music, art, dreams, joys, and regrets . . . all the adventures that make life rich and meaningful. I dearly loved this woman, and she had a huge impact on my life.

Two days before she died, I called Joanne to visit a bit, not realizing death was so near. When I told the person who answered who I was, she said, "Oh yes . . . Joanne wants to talk with you." In a very weak, barely audible voice, my friend said, "Luci, you are a gift to the whole world. Thank you for being in my life"—then handed the phone back to her caregiver.

I cried when I heard Joanne's voice, knowing she probably wouldn't last long in that weakened condition. And I'll never forget her words, or that enormous compliment. But it was a great deal more to me than an expression of kindness. It was God's injunction through the soft, sweet voice of Joanne. He was saying, "I have given you life, Luci. It's a gift. Now I want you to live that life by embracing the whole world."

God has put the world on my heart—he's put it on all our hearts. His desire is that we would go into it—in whatever way we can. He has a gift for the entire world, and it is in us, his people.

Every person is a combination of many factors woven together from the joys and sorrows of life. We're also the product of our choices. We're the result of what was or was not done for or to us by our parents, siblings, associates, and friends. The journey we're on is planned and watched over by a loving God who wants us to treasure the gift of being alive and who sets us free to participate in our own destiny. Embracing that journey—whatever it is for each of us, wherever it takes us—is imperative to capturing the spirit of adventure.

When we realize our lives are to be given away, everything about our outlook changes and grows. God takes our youth and gives us in exchange his truth. We see and do things differently as a result. We think beyond our own borders. The world becomes accessible through the power of God's Spirit and love. We capture each moment, embrace the journey, and go forward.

Never look down to test the ground before taking your next step:
only he who keeps his eye fixed on the far horizon will find his right road.

—*Dag Hammarskjöld*

_____

_____

_____

_____

_____

_____

_____

_____

_____

_____

_____

_____

_____

_____

_____

_____

_____

Adventure starts in the mind then travels to the heart. If it lodges there long enough, it heads to the ticket counter, gets on a plane, and flies away. Where have you never been—"out there" or inside—that beckons you? How can you let the spirit of adventure take you there?

There are days when we're so happy our feet don't touch the ground.
Describe a day when your feet didn't touch the ground.

_____

_____

_____

_____

_____

_____

_____

_____

_____

_____

_____

_____

_____

_____

_____

_____

_____

_____

If I don't dream it and think about it and plan it, nothing will happen.
List your dreams and keep coming back to these pages to fill in your plans.
Make your dreams happen.

A Pocket Park - A Place of Grace -
a hang-out, a safe place for the girls + women
of Terlingua.

If I don't plan it + work the plan, it won't happen.

PART 2

CAPTURING THE MOMENT

Nikon

·3.3 Mega-
pixels
·2.5x Zoom
·5 Area
Multi-
Autofocus

FRONT

NIKON COOLPIX 880 DIGITAL
w/8-20mm Zoom NIKKOR

There's a lovely old castle on the banks of the Danube where I spent a week's vacation a few years ago. Schloss Dürnstein! A magical place in a dazzling location. Tucked into high cliffs overlooking one of the most beautiful scenes in Austria, this castle (built in 1630) has a garden terrace where tables are set up under the trees. Guests take all their meals there, enjoying outstanding food and wine while watching the river activities: swimmers, boats, barges. It's heaven on earth. All I did for a full week was sleep, eat, take pictures, read, and paint. Oh . . . and write postcards. I'm crazy about postcards. During my first trip to Europe, I wrote sixty-one cards. About three a day.

A few months before leaving for Austria, my friend and colleague Patsy Clairmont introduced me to the Toot and Puddle children's books by Holly Hobbie—about two friends who live together in Woodcock Pocket. Toot wants to see the world, but Puddle prefers staying home. They are charming little pigs dressed in appropriate attire characterizing their preferences. Toot wears traveling shorts, hat, and a backpack, while Puddle has on a pair of denim overalls and a ball cap. Throughout the book they exchange postcards about the activities of their days while apart from each other. Terribly clever! I had found the dolls that go with the books and had given them to Patsy as a gift.

Well, nothing would do but that Toot go with me to Austria. Patsy packed him up, put a quarter in his backpack, and I stuck him in my carry-on. Each day of my trip Toot wrote Puddle a card. He dreamed up all kinds of things to say, and I photographed him in various settings. When I sat at the big window overlooking the Danube, painting vineyards and little houses in the distance, Toot was there looking at the same thing. I even water-colored a postcard, one that he sent to Puddle. Toot had a great time, and so did I. At the end of the trip, I made a calendar for Patsy with twelve pictures of Toot in different Austrian settings (one for each month)—in flower gardens, museums, the window of the castle, choosing postcards, and finally . . . tucked in bed—a fun project that enabled Patsy to take the trip with me vicariously.

Postcards are one of the simplest and greatest ways in the world to capture the moment. They're colorful, easy to acquire, quick to write, and inexpensive. In a few minutes' time you tell somebody on the other side of the world that you love her and are thinking of her. I write cards all the time, even from home. Wrote one last night to one of my Texas pals.

I've written postcards to myself too. On a trip to South America, my friends and I wrote two different postcards addressed to me. I gave one of them and a five-dollar bill to the guide on our bus (Andrea Hernández, from Punta Arenas, Chile), suggesting she add something herself, buy a stamp, and mail the card when she finished. "I hope this isn't too much trouble," I said, handing her the money and our already written card.

"No trouble at all. I'm honored," she said.

"If there's any money left over, have a cup of coffee on me." I strolled away, wondering if she'd do it.

Shortly after I got home, the postcard came. In fact, Andrea had not only added a few lines but also put it in a stamped envelope to keep it safe and clean before dropping it in the mail. In small, very legible handwriting, she wrote:

Hello Lady!!

I'm Andrea, your guide. Do you remember me? This is an unforgettable treasure to you, so I'm enclosing a bit of my loving to Palm Desert from a country which is waiting for you. I hope you keep this forever and thanks a lot for being such a nice and lovely lady. An advice to you: never stop on dreaming! Thank you again for trust in me!

Andrea Hernández. Punta Arenas

Andrea honey, be sure of this: I'll never part with that card, and I'll never "stop on dreaming." Not on your life!

When I saw the Taj Mahal in India, a place I had wanted to go since childhood, I asked the friends with whom I was traveling to add to the card

I had written to myself. They did, we all signed it, I mailed it, and bingo!—it arrived after I got home. I was a happy girl with a treasured memory right in the palm of my hand.

Moments come and go so fast, but they are what make up the whole of life. Little bitty moments here and there. They turn into hours and days and weeks—ultimately an entire lifetime. When I consciously think about that, it makes me want to slow down. Sometimes I can't slow down. I don't have the time to go slowly. But I can capture a moment in a postcard or photograph. Then, years later it all comes back to me as a sweet gift to myself.

Life is short and everything is irrevocable. No matter what we do to lengthen the moment, we can't. No matter how eager we are to shorten uncomfortable events, that can't be done either. If we don't learn to live fully in the present, much of life passes us by, lost in the cobwebs of time forever, often unremembered. The passage of time can't be retrieved except in our memory banks. That's why we must be all there at any given moment. Even during the times that are frightening or difficult. Everything has a purpose, and if we don't want to miss that purpose and the adventure along the way, then we must be conscious, alert, curious, openhearted. When we capture the moment we're in, we're fully alive.

Perhaps you remember the *New Yorker* cartoon in which two monks in robes and shaved heads are sitting side by side, cross-legged on the floor. The younger one, with a quizzical look on his face, is facing the older, who is saying: "Nothing happens next. This is it."

That's exactly what it means to live in the here and now. We aren't waiting for something else to occur, we aren't distracted by anything around us, and we aren't trying to escape mentally to another time. We are "mindfully awake." Paying attention. Savoring the moment for all it's worth. We are fully alive!

I once heard Diane Sawyer say on television, "The most important thing in life is to pay attention"—and I would agree. But how often are we able to achieve that? Not often enough, unfortunately. Nevertheless, our richest times in life are those when we are completely present, consciously heightening our awareness because our journey has brought us here—and we choose not to miss it.

I feel this when I'm engaged in rich, meaningful conversation with an interesting person. Questions are enticing, listening is acute, and eye contact is direct. I love that; such focused attention makes me feel alive. I also experience this feeling when I'm alone . . . in an art museum or lost in a good book. When I'm all there—or rather, all here!—I never want the moment to end. It's as though I can actually hear my heart beat—my very own heart, which sustains the life I'm living. I'm breathing. I'm feeling myself breathe . . . in and out, in and out. It's wonderful. It's this moment. It's the "it" to which the wise old monk referred.

About a year after my mother died in 1971, my dad and I were invited to the wedding of a mutual friend. Daddy was living with Chuck and his family, and I picked him up so we could go in my car. At the age of seventy-eight, he wasn't driving anymore. Since we had more time than expected, I suggested we stop for coffee on the way at a little short-order house where we knew a couple of the waitresses. Here we were, dressed to the nines, leaving our wedding gift in the car and going into this little dump of a place for coffee. I thought it was a fun little adventure and would be an enjoyable detour for Daddy.

Before long, it began to rain, so we decided to let the weather clear up before we traveled on. As we settled back into our chairs, Daddy and I began to have the most wonderful conversation. I asked him about his childhood, his parents, his brother, his work, and so on. We talked about Mother and his love for her through the forty years they were married. He told me how hard it was when she died so unexpectedly and wondered why the Lord hadn't taken him first since he was fifteen years older than she. Daddy was so sweet (as always) and vulnerable that evening. He was totally engaged and mindful, not distracted by anything at all.

I thanked him for being such a great dad through the years and for always showing me such respect, support, and love. We talked about my brothers and what it was like for Daddy to be a father with the financial responsibilities that were his when the three of us were growing up. We were totally connected conversationally, and the time seemed to fly.

All the while, it rained harder and harder. Finally, we gave up the idea of going to the wedding altogether and nestled in to one of the sweetest times my dad and I ever had. All my life we were close, but never more than that night. I asked Daddy to forgive me when, in childhood, I got mad at him when he disciplined me or didn't do things my way. Oh my . . . just thinking back on that heartfelt exchange makes me tearful all over again. My dad and I were totally present, totally real, absolutely in the moment and connected.

After a couple of hours, the waitresses we knew came over and joined us. Since nobody was coming in for service during the downpour, they sat down, listened to our stories and escapades, and even entered into our conversation, which by this time had turned into laughter and nuttiness. Daddy told jokes. We laughed. Then I'd tell one or two. We began talking about music and singing, and before long all of us were singing . . . patriotic songs, campfire tunes, little ditties everybody knew. The waitresses left after a bit and came back with bacon and eggs for Daddy and me. By this time it must have been ten o'clock, and we couldn't imagine where the time had gone. I mentioned that Daddy used to play the harmonica, and before long somebody produced one and Daddy played it. What a fun night! What a memory.

Would that we were able to maintain that kind of connectedness all the time, with others as well as with ourselves. It's hard, almost impossible. So often we want to be somewhere else. When we look at the Now we are in, we have the illusion that if we could just inch or leap forward on the journey, our lives would be richer or better or more "together." We don't want to be here.

It's like the piece I saw in a "Dear Abby" column years ago, written by a young man named Jason Lehman. At the age of only fourteen, he wrote the most wonderful and poignant expression of my thoughts, called "Present Tense."

> It was spring . . . but it was summer I wanted,
> the warm days, and the great outdoors.
> It was summer, but it was fall I wanted,
> the colorful leaves, and the cool, dry air.
> It was fall, but it was winter I wanted,
> the beautiful snow, and the holiday season.
> It was winter, but it was spring I wanted,
> the warmth, and the blossoming of nature.
> I was a child, but it was adulthood I wanted,
> the freedom, and the respect.
> I was 20, but it was 30 I wanted,
> to be mature, and sophisticated.
> I was middle-aged, but it was 20 I wanted,
> the youth, and the free spirit.
> I was retired, but it was middle age I wanted,
> the presence of mind, without limitations.
> My life was over. But I never got what I wanted.[4]

My, oh my! I've shared those words with others and listened to them say, "A fourteen-year-old couldn't have written that." But I believe he could have. The desire to be older or younger or different or someplace else instead of who we are, when we are, and where we are seems to be the perennial cry of all human hearts, no matter our age. As the psalmist lamented,

> *Oh, that I had the wings of a dove!*
> *I would fly away and be at rest—*
> *I would flee far away*
> *and stay in the desert;*
> *I would hurry to my place of shelter,*
> *far from the tempest and storm. (Psalm 55:6–8)*

The poet William Sharp echoed that deep human desire to seek solace and fulfillment somewhere other than here: "My heart is a lonely hunter that hunts on a lonely hill." The human heart quests for satisfaction and keeps at it until it finds some kind of peace in God. Until that day we say, in effect, "It has to be better over there"—and "over there" can be virtually anywhere. And even when we find contentedness in the Lord and know for a fact that he is our constant companion, it's still difficult for the heart to give up the hunt. Why is this? Why are we made like this? Why are we so rarely satisfied? Were we simply programmed to be this way, or is it that we just don't know ourselves or God well enough to recognize what truly satisfies? Is it in front of our nose and we can't see it?

As I look back over my own life, there were many times I wasn't satisfied; I couldn't live fully in the moment. I kept thinking there was something more or something better just over the next hill. I was always looking for the next thing to bring me fulfillment and, of course, I wanted that fulfillment to be permanent. I wanted to find it, be happy with it, put it to rest, and never have to search again. I didn't want my own heart to be a lonely hunter. Who does?

One of the hardest periods in my life was in the mid-eighties. It ultimately became one of the most transforming times because I was willing to attune myself fully to the here and now—even though it was painful. It turned out that my own discomfort contained critical information that formed a pathway to the next leg of my journey. But it was very hard to be as vulnerable as I needed to be to see the real roadblock.

I had experienced some heartbreaking misunderstandings with close friends and had narrowed my circle of meaningful relationships to only a few. At the same time, I was trying to make a major decision—whether to take early retirement from Mobil because of the impending collision between my "real" job and lots of speaking engagements. My insides cried out for cohesiveness and order. I wanted to scream "Stop!" to somebody. I felt these feelings every morning when I awakened and every night when I went to bed. It was an overriding pain that never went away. Some days it wasn't as noticeable because of lots of activity, but it was never quite fixed. I couldn't figure out what was wrong.

When I had had enough of these feelings, I decided to turn the whole thing over to God, to pray fervently about the problems I was aware of, and try my best to leave the whole knotted skein of turmoil with him. As days and weeks passed, it seemed as though I heard in my head, "Write things down." It wasn't a big message in neon lights; it was a nudge in my spirit, like a little voice encouraging me to set down in black and white the actual things that were driving me nuts. "Please take notes." So, I did.

The first thing I wrote was a letter to myself on August 1, 1985. I still have it and have reread it a dozen times or more, always jotting the new reading date at the bottom. It also served as a prayer from the deepest part of my heart, and it begins like this:

I am writing this at 4:30 a.m. because I can't sleep. What concerns me lies so heavily on my mind it's keeping me awake. I want to write down what's going through my thoughts, for clarification. Right now, here in my bedroom I feel like I'm the only person in the world. I feel very alone. At the moment, I don't feel as lonely as I do "alone," because in a few hours I'll go to work and be out in the swim of activity. My sitting here, writing, is a temporary thing. But basically, down deep inside I am lonely. That's what concerns me. It all falls under the broad topic of "what am I going to do about being so lonely?" Do I want to try and change it? To what degree? How?

Let me try to explain this to myself . . . to walk through all the steps, in detail. Writing about something is a great catharsis to me. I need to get a better grip on this as well as try and understand what God might be trying to show me or to teach me at this period in my life. I want to be sensitive to him, in case there is a message in all of this to change the course of my life, or at least so that I'm cognizant of the "value" and reason for these feelings. Let me be as honest and open as I can . . .

I went on to outline the feelings I had that morning and what I'd been dealing with for months or, perhaps unknowingly, for years. I wrote about goals I had and wanted to achieve. I named some of my closest friends and how far I felt from them emotionally or geographically. I listed the persons who fit most deeply in the picture and why—how I expected certain things from them and they didn't come through. Some had moved away and broken my heart. I felt bereft.

Then I listed the things I was grateful for: my health, my job, opportunities to travel, books I had in print and the prospect for more writing. All academic things—no people that made me really happy. I talked about the one person who had so deeply disappointed me because I was giving more in the relationship than that individual was giving back. I cried out to God in that letter and exposed all my anger, fears, regrets, inadequacies, fault-finding, dread, and despair.

Then I wrote the question, What can I do about it? As the Holy Spirit brought things to mind, I made a list of ten ideas I thought might make a difference. I was very honest, embarrassingly so, and five pages later I stopped writing and went back to bed. For the first time in weeks, I slept soundly. Everything that had been inside was now outside. It had a body of its own and was no longer this floating, fearful specter that had been hovering over me, wreaking havoc in my soul. Right in front of me was the dilemma—to read, look at, think and pray about, and even refer to in years to come. I had dumped it all on the only one who could handle the whole truckload. I was that broken in my grief, and he was that touched in his mercy. I felt it; I knew it; and for the first time in months, my burden seemed a little lighter.

As the weeks passed and I continually prayed about this whole situation, positive things began to happen. First of all, I began to realize that one of my most annoying problems was me. That was painfully revealing. How could I be my own problem? Simple: I wanted control. Control of everything! I resented the fact that God wanted control too. My desire for control outweighed my desire for connectedness, even with him. I never saw that glaring defect in my own character until I wrote down what I'd been feeling. I was unable to recognize that I was a big part of the problem, not just these other people. I felt lonely because I had attached all the desires of my heart to a tiny circle of friends and companions from whom I wanted all my needs met, and they just happened to have lives of their own! I had completely taken my eyes off the big picture of what God had in store for me. I didn't want the life I was living then; I wanted some pie-in-the-sky existence that wasn't possible, and for some reason I was holding out for it before I would permit myself to be happy where I was. I'd show God! Of course, that wasn't written out, but it was definitely underneath my feelings of despair.

That letter became not only a place to see in stark relief what my true trouble was, but a mirror that reflected back to me how essential it was to live in the present moment, to live fully where I was, to wait on God himself to open doors, to stop controlling other people and their decisions!

Second, in September of that same year, I wrote down a list of goals and priorities. They had to do with all the things I felt were important in life . . . for now and for later. (I still have that list . . . pack rats save everything.) The first thing I wanted to do was determine if and when I could retire from Mobil. This list was figured on a three-year plan: September 1, 1985, to September 1, 1988. It aimed for a September 1, 1988, retirement date. Here's what I asked of myself:

- *Have car sold and new one bought.*
- *Have two more books published.*

- *Take one more trip abroad.*
- *Have my Keogh plan paid up.*
- *Investigate retirement fund rollover.*
- *Have all my classical music categorized.*
- *Design a reading program for myself.*
- *Look into moving . . . buying? Renting?*
- *Have a garage sale.*
- *Have idea for a new book.*
- *Have at least five out-of-state speaking engagements on the calendar.*
- *Have a regular Bible study.*
- *Create a Scripture memory program.*
- *Have a strong tithing program.*
- *Subscribe to the* New York Times.
- *Visit more art museums, everywhere in the world.*
- *Cook more meals at home.*
- *Quit griping. Grow up.*

There were big goals as well as small ones, but each had as an objective to stretch me and enlarge my borders. They gave organization and structure. These were worthy things I could actually aim toward and achieve over time. Nothing was too far "out there," but all of it took discipline—something I was lacking when I felt so frightened. But notice, this entire list was about things, not people. Hmmm . . . I was still disconnected from my deepest need, it seemed.

The third thing I did was what rounded me toward home plate. I had been to a Mobil management meeting where I picked up a magazine called the *Executive Female*. In that January/February 1986 issue there was an article entitled "Plot Your Lifeline." I read it and thought the suggested exercise looked important to my scheme of things. It was thought provoking.

Basically, this was a graph on which one could chart one's life journey, including both personal and career experiences. There was a mean line in the middle marked with a "0," above which were all the + and ++ marks. In this space I was to plot happenings in my life that were positive or very positive. And below the zero line were minus and double minus marks, where the less-than-positive and painful happenings occurred. The graph started at age one and went out as far as ninety in increments of five years. I marked my age at fifty-four and began plotting. Some interesting data quickly emerged.

For the most part I had enjoyed a life of success—happy childhood, graduation from high school and college, meaningful relationships, professional singing, good career with promotions along the way, strong God-consciousness, books published, travel, and so forth. By anyone's standards, each of these was a worthy achievement, and I, a happy, fulfilled person. Above the mean line there were many pluses.

But below the zero line there were three very difficult experiences that had indented my soul. One was the pain of individuation related to those early problems with my mother—the hurt and sorrow between us that had taken its toll because of my inability to please her no matter how hard I tried. The second was my move from Texas to California in the early seventies when I felt like a fish out of water and it took me at least two years to find a place of emotional stability. And the third was this current time of loneliness, brought on by insisting things go as I wanted them to.

I looked at the chart carefully and realized something that changed me deeply from that moment on: it was these three "double-minus" experiences that had given me my greatest strength and fiber—what I most needed to mature. Through them I was forced to rely on the Lord, deal with reality for what it was, defer reward—in short, quit griping and grow up! The very things I hated had been the making of me. It was as if I took off a blindfold and walked into the light.

While I had enjoyed all the things in the plus category and had had lots of fun, there was no suffering or heartache there—nothing to build character or to necessarily provide the richest fodder needed for becoming a balanced adult. Nothing to extract from me the deepest, most revealing, and most transforming truths about myself. These below-zero experiences had actually helped me the most to become the person God wanted me to be. When the exercise was finished, I felt as if I had hit a home run. I felt truly alive and had the guidance I needed to finally take constructive action in my life.

The soul in each of us is imprisoned until it is set free by Jesus Christ. We all have shells around us, protecting us from being eaten alive by the pain of life. And when those shells break, we believe we are at grave risk of being hurt, depressed, or even dying on the spot. To prevent this pain and loss, we guard ourselves by retreating deeper and deeper into the shell, being available only to what is pleasant, predictable, and safe.

But every person I've ever known who really had something to give has been burst open by the explosive force of God's soul-transforming lessons. They have each been willing to be vulnerable to the truth about themselves, to admit selfishness and behavior patterns that are maddening to other people and destructive to their own souls. Bursting out of a shell means walls down, roofs off to our feelings. If we aspire to pay complete attention to the present, we must stay connected to our individual centers and at the same time get out of our own ways. Living fully in the present starts deep inside as we allow the self-protective shell to break open so the liberating grace of God can flow in to heal and renew and establish genuine meaning in our lives.

On September 1, 1987, I retired from Mobil Oil Corporation—one year earlier than I had planned. And I had achieved almost everything on my long list. Most important, some of the relationships I had agonized over had also been restored. They weren't even on the list. How could God work without a list? Amazing grace! When I went to my retirement party, I kept thinking of these Scriptures, which I had memorized long before:

"With man this is impossible, but with God all things are possible."
(Matthew 19:26)

"Until now you have not asked for anything in my name. Ask and you will receive, and your joy will be complete." (John 16:24)

*And my God will meet all your needs according to his glorious riches
in Christ Jesus. To our God and Father be glory for ever and ever.
Amen. (Philippians 4:19–20)*

For a short period of time, I worked as vice president of public rela-
tions at Insight for Living, the international radio Bible ministry of my
brother Chuck. While that was a unique and meaningful opportunity to be
with my family as well as transition out of the corporate world, I found I
spent more time traveling and speaking than I did working in the office. As
I once again faced the fact that I was not quite in the place the Lord wanted
me, I asked for his direction in helping me decide what to do. Insight for
Living needed a full-time employee, and I needed relief from trying to be
two places at once.

In the spring of 1992, I had so many dates on my calendar to speak that
I decided to once again "retire" (if there is such a thing) from an office job
and trust the Lord to meet my financial needs on his own terms. Get out of
your way, Lucille. Oh, how often have I said that?

It hadn't occurred to me that the Lord would keep bringing me all kinds
of unexpected opportunities year after year, once I left an eight-to-five job.
I had always worked in an office, drawn a paycheck from an office, and was
so accustomed to that kind of structure I couldn't seem to think outside that
box. But God could. Immediately, I had more speaking engagements and
writing opportunities than I could handle, and the days ran into weeks and
the weeks into months and years.

It was actually kind of funny, because in some early conversations with
my financial advisers, they had determined I had enough money to live
until age eighty-four; then I would have to die. Or they'd have to shoot me!
We've laughed at that forecast more than once because we've discovered
that God had so much more in mind.

In the latter part of 1995, I received an invitation to speak at several conferences the following year. The conference organization (which has become
widely known as Women of Faith) was founded by author and entrepreneur
Stephen Arterburn and was designed to be a source of encouragement to

women across America. Steve wanted women to have fun, get away from their routines for a weekend, and sing and worship the Lord with other women. With this vision as a springboard, he contacted four speakers and asked if we were available. I was one of those four, along with Patsy Clairmont, Marilyn Meberg, and Barbara Johnson. "Make 'em laugh!" was more or less our instruction when we first began. We were all busy with our own ministries, but because we knew and loved each other, we all said yes to doing eight "Joyful Journey" conferences around the nation. The following year (1997), Steve invited Thelma Wells and Sheila Walsh to join the team. We loved them right off the bat. They fit right in with our wackiness and spirit of adventure!

the Women of Faith
Speaking Team —

is
controls
rified: DAILY."

= Salvation Verses
= Connecting or significant
  words or phrases.
= anthropopathisms. (feelings)
= anthropomorphism: (forms)
= aorist tense; Greek "if."
= linear action; punctiliar action
= Satanic references or truths
  Words: opposite of the Truth
R.P.T. = Retroactive Positional Truth
P.T. = Positional Truth
E.F. = Eternal Fellowship
T.F. = Temporal Fellowship
L.A. = Linear action
P.A. = Punctiliar action
M.A. = Mental Attitude
O.S.N. = Old Sin Nature
D.V.P. = Divine View Point
H.V.P. = Human View Point
Greek "if."
Phil.2:1-if: (1st class condition)
  and it is true
Gal.3:21-if: (2nd class condition)
  and it is not true
I John1:9-if: (3rd class condition)
  maybe it is true; maybe it's not
I Peter 3:14-if: (4th class condition)
  I wish it were true, but it's

Stems of Hebrew verbs:
① Cal- meant simply to do it."
② Ni-fel- Reflective action... it was done to them
③ Hith-pa-el - Had to it themselves and no
  oneelse could do it for them. Lev.5:5

And God was doing something—we could feel it! Every time we spoke at another venue, we experienced fresh excitement. Thousands of women were discovering what it meant to be a "woman of faith," to trust God with their desires, their families, their problems, their lives. Talk about adventure!

We've spoken to four million women in the past fourteen years. Who in the world ever would have imagined the numerous doors Women of Faith would open for all of us? I, for one, didn't even dream that God would swing open this door—a wonderful, exciting way to come together with fabulous women I love and admire for a common purpose that has eternal value. We tell our stories, worship together, and pray for each other and the women in our audience. We travel around the United States and the world, reaching the people God has ordained to cross our paths. It's all in his hands, and we just keep showing up.

We never know how things will turn out, do we? Feeling stuck or overwhelmed makes us despondent and causes us to stay put a lot longer than we need to. But for me, writing that predawn letter so many years ago taught me things I'll never forget. Once I saw my effrontery and self-centeredness on paper and could finally decipher the magnitude of my control problem, I knew change was necessary—and, with Christ, possible. I believed I could trust the God of the universe to reveal a new path before me, one step at a time.

God has shown me that wherever I am in life can be my very best place. I had no idea all the things he had in mind for my future. Had he told me years ago what was ahead, I wouldn't have believed him anyway. He was going to take me on wonderful adventures from here to there—to destinations both within my own soul and outside in the wide world that I never dreamed of! That list I made in September 1985 was only a drop in the bucket to all he had in mind for my journey. And I'm still movin'!

Drink in life and savor every drop—the sweet and the sour,
the good and the bad, the planned and the unplanned.
When you do, you'll feel fully alive.

_____

_____

_____

_____

_____

_____

_____

_____

_____

_____

_____

_____

_____

_____

_____

_____

_____

Embracing the moment is a choice, a way of life.
It requires us to be awake, mindful of the present.

Charles
Lovell
Lucille
Orville
Party

If we don't fully live in the moment, there's no rewinding or playing forward that assures us of a better day. But to live in the moment we have to realize for every good day there's a bad day . . . every zenith has a nadir. If we experience happiness, we're able to do that because we have known sadness. If we experience good health, we enjoy it more having known sickness. The ability to feel anything is based on the degree to which we experience its opposite. What have you learned on a bad day that helped you enjoy a good day?

_____

_____

_____

_____

_____

_____

_____

_____

_____

_____

_____

_____

_____

_____

_____

Much about human nature is understandable, forthright, and clear, but there are things that we'll never understand, no matter how well we get to know ourselves. How often have you said, "Why in the world did I do that?" Write about a time you asked yourself that question.

_____

_____

_____

_____

_____

_____

_____

_____

_____

_____

_____

_____

_____

_____

_____

_____

_____

_____

_____

If I had all the money in the world, I'd go to Africa every year. Without exception. That is the most interesting place I've ever visited. Adventure abounds! Behind every bush there is something exciting to see. I've been nine times and have hardly scratched the surface.

On each of those trips I went with my favorite traveling companion, Mary Graham. The first time Mary and I "did Africa" together was 1996. In my usual Melvin Udall way, I mapped out the trip for months. Sometime in the late '80s I bought a big, fat, ten-ton book called *The African Safari—the Ultimate Wildlife and Photographic Adventure*, and it was, indeed, the "ultimate." It was almost too heavy to lift, so I couldn't take it very far from home, but I read it whenever I could. I studied all the places where it looked like we'd see the most game and get the best photos, and together, out of that vast continent of offerings, we chose Kenya. We determined the best season to go and began mapping out a workable trip.

Years before I had read *Out of Africa* by Isak Dinesen (one of the best books ever written), *Born Free* by Joy Adamson, *The Africa of Albert Schweitzer* by Charles Joy and Melvin Arnold, *I Dreamed of Africa* by Kuki Gallmann, and *West with the Night* by Beryl Markham, and I was in the process of devouring (page by page) that descriptive and colorfully written old book by Theodore Roosevelt, *African Game Trails*. Incidentally, anybody who travels to Africa should read all of these, but especially the Roosevelt book. Even though it has to do with killing wild game (I don't approve), it's a fantastic account of the African wanderings of this great man and his son Kermit.

As I dreamed of Africa myself, I outlined an itinerary for our trip on my computer, drew a map of what to do when and where, and on August 8, Mary and I were on our way to London, the first leg of our adventure. After a couple of delightful days in London, it was time to fly to Nairobi. By now I was hyperventilating. Mary said, "For the first time you look like you fit in, Luci—tripod hanging off your backpack, camera off your shoulder, vest, safari hat, scarf around your neck."

All exchanges for
US Travelers cheques —
To British £
and
Kenya shillings

"You noticed?"

Everybody at the departure gate looked like me. Roll-ons, backpacks, and camera equipment coming out the wazoo. I just know some of those guys worked for *National Geographic*. I never saw such powerful lenses in my life. And they carried them like they were babies. I understood.

It's hard to sleep and hyperventilate at the same time. Mary was out for most of the all-night flight, but I read, wrote in my journal, walked around, ordered numerous cups of hot tea, and learned how to say, "Have you seen a lion?" in Swahili.

We were on our way.

We landed in Nairobi, the capital of Kenya. Anybody who goes to East Africa passes through Nairobi. It is large and dirty and third world and full of enormous government problems, and I love it. The leading cause of death in Kenya is highway accidents, and the overcrowded matatus (city buses) in Nairobi don't help any. Generally speaking, it's in a constant state of upheaval, but when I walked off the plane, I saw Shangri-la.

We were met by a friend of Mary's, Julie Mumley, who drove us to her home where we met her wonderful family. The Mumleys are Americans who have lived in Africa a number of years. They are warm, friendly, and helpful. They drove us to Wilson Airport, and in a matter of minutes we were chugging and bumping toward the Serengeti in the world's tiniest plane with a pilot who was doing all sorts of stunts.

"New at this?" I asked.

"Naw, I do this every day. Been here twice this morning as a matter of fact. This your first time in Kenya?"

I told him it was and that I was beside myself with excitement.

"Oh . . . you'll love it," he said. "A safari is the greatest adventure in the world." At that moment a giraffe ran under the plane—right where we were to land—and I knew I was hooked forever.

There aren't many things I enjoy as much on repeat performance, but an

African safari is one of them. It is unique every time. And here's what's weird: I'm not really an animal lover, but these wild, unpredictable creatures have stolen my heart. One simply cannot foresee what they will do. They're full of surprises! They show up where least expected in unbelievable diversity, fill the night air with strange noises, take on one another in savage combat, and give the viewer hours of contemplation and photographic opportunities.

And it's not only the animals that lure me back. It's Africa itself: mysterious, melancholy, untamed, and vast. When I awake in the morning, there is no other silence like that. When I face the day, there's no dawn like that. When I go to bed at night, there's neither more glorious moon nor more splendid stars than those. So many unexplored landscapes beckon. Just listening to the grasses rustle in the soft breeze helps me rest and forget everything else. In some strange way, I experience complete harmony with life and I feel at home.

The African people have a gentle flow about them, a sense of individuality and inborn stillness. Their pace reminds me of my childhood in Texas. By nature, Texans are deliberate, methodical, and downright slow at times. I know I am. I hate to hurry. It goes against my grain. My friends tease me about being this way, but it doesn't bother me. (Maybe I'm so slow it doesn't register.) It's the way I grew up. Ever seen one of those old movies where all the cowboys in the poker game have this studied look, hoping to outguess the other, waiting for someone else to lay his hand down first? They know when to hold 'em and when to fold 'em.

This is the way it is on safari. Quiet. Calm. Studied. Holdin' and foldin'. I can feel my brain ticking and thoughts developing in the quietness of the moment. I love that. And I love it most when I have a camera in my hand.

We Americans have lost our ability to be still. If we don't rush, we miss the boat. If we don't have a cell phone, beeper, laptop, and pager, we feel we can't accomplish anything. But in Africa . . . who cares about accomplishing things?

During a safari, it's not possible to have my own way. This is another thing I like. I have to go with the flow of the undomesticated animals if I want to see them and capture them on film. I must move gently, falling in with the wind and the colors and the smells of where I am. In short, I must wait.

I remember leaving camp early one morning in the Land Rover with my buddies and our guide when, in a matter of minutes, we encountered a mother cheetah with two cubs. They were so fascinating to watch in the first light of dawn. The cubs pranced around, galloping here and there, batting each other's faces, having the best time, when suddenly the mother spotted a herd of impala grazing just ahead of us down the road. Everything changed. We pulled to a complete stop. The cubs instinctively stood dead still as the mother fixed her gaze. Breakfast! Our chatting ceased. I could hear my heart beating.

For at least twenty minutes, those cheetah cubs never twitched a muscle as their mother planned her move. She crouched in the road—low, lower,

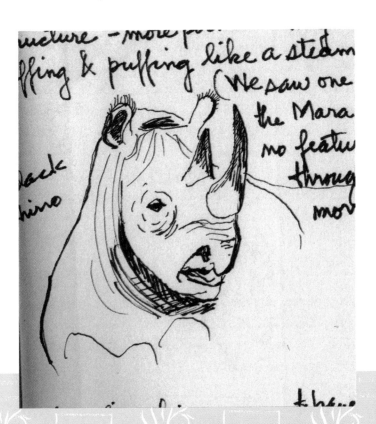

lowest—until she almost disappeared. Finally, one of the impalas got separated from the herd and—*spring!*—Mama was off and running.

Cheetahs are amazing animals. They may not have powerful jaws or the ability to drag their prey or climb trees, but can they run! The cheetah is the fastest land animal on earth, streaking across the plains at seventy miles per hour. This lethal sprint is its greatest hunting weapon, and this is why a cheetah is so fun to watch. Its flexible spine goes into gear, then, like a spring, it uncoils, the legs shoot out, and the cheetah takes off with the longest stride in the cat world.

I put down my camera to watch the drama—up and down the hills, through high grass and low gullies the cheetah and impala ran. Nobody took pictures because the subjects weren't still long enough. The impala ultimately got away, and a very tired cheetah mother returned to her cubs with no breakfast. She lay down, panting and resting after that long, fruitless run. Then, and only then, did the little cubs resume their playing as life went on in the wilds of Kenya.

As we drove away, I realized we would have missed that whole drama had we been in a hurry. That mama cheetah would never have attempted her run had her children not known the tempo of the game. This is the rhythm of life in Africa. Some days you win; some days you lose. Some days the predator takes the spoils; other days she loses the spoils. In everything, one must be, in Isak Dinesen's words, on "friendly terms with time."

The most difficult wild animal to see in Africa is the leopard. I know people who have lived there for decades and never seen one. Leopards are my favorite of the cat family because they are rare, solitary, nocturnal, and beautiful. It does no good to listen for them, because there's not much to hear. Their mouth noises are described as a quiet hiss or growl, a rasping yowl or a cough. Leopards never roar. They are utterly silent except for these telltale throat sounds. Not only are they silent, but they're patient. Characteristically, a leopard slinks, creeps, or belly-crawls toward its prey. Then it strikes like lightning—graceful, precise . . . deadly. It hauls its kill up in the crook of a tree to eat at leisure without interruption. It's the smallest of the big cats—a compact powerhouse.

On our first trip to Africa, Mary and I had been warned not to get our hopes up about seeing the elusive leopard. Okay, fine. *Hakuna matata.* We had resigned ourselves to that probability even though we prayed every night that God would drop one in our laps . . . so to speak. And if we had come home without seeing one, we would have been two ecstatic campers because of all the marvelous animals we did see.

But guess what? We saw two . . . in one afternoon. There aren't enough words to tell you the thrill of that. I took four rolls of film right on the spot, with three different cameras. I was snapping one while Mary was loading another, and we were both so emotionally intoxicated we could hardly breathe. But I'm ahead of myself.

It was the last fifteen minutes of the last game drive of our last day on safari in the Aberdares National Park, and we were with Silas, a personable Kenyan driver/guide. This park is noted for its large, lush, protected rain-forest of dense vegetation and red earth, rich in iron ore. It was like being inside a gigantic George Inness painting—all green, then a swath of red cut across the middle. Everything was wet with rain, and the animals were terri-bly hard to see because there was so much thick foliage. This particular park doesn't permit vehicles to leave the road (as they do in the Serengeti), so we rolled along—*pole pole* (slowly, slowly)—chatting as we headed toward the gate to leave, having seen very little in our three-hour safari.

Silas had stopped the car momentarily so he could use his hands while answering one of our many questions, when suddenly a beautiful leopard walked right out of the forest, crossed in front of us, and sat down on the side of the road. He wasn't six feet from us. I stared in disbelief as we all pointed, whispered, and quietly lost our minds. It was one of the best moments of my life! *Click. Click. Click. Click.* My camera went crazy.

I changed lenses, film, expressions, and moods so fast one would have thought I was schizophrenic—unable to function within the limits of my normal personality. I was literally beside myself. I said things that made no sense. I talked to the leopard: "Turn left. Please. Can you scratch your ear? Walk across in front of me so I can get a better picture." And, amazingly, he did everything I asked. Thanks.

Then, as if that wasn't enough, just as the first leopard found a spot to lie down on our right, a second one came out of the bushes, crossed the road to the left, and did exactly as the first had done, as if they were obeying a circus trainer who had been left back in the bush. "You go out there and do what your brother did, and I'll give you a nice fat gazelle for dinner." And he did.

Within a ten-minute span, I captured on film one of the finest moments anyone's ever had on safari. I have it all on film. Lots and lots of film! And written in my journal. Lots and lots of pages! If I never see another leopard, this singular moment is mine forever. I am totally satisfied with that gift the Lord gave me. There were only five of us there that day: a handsome Kenyan national who loved his country and was so proud to show off its best, my dearest traveling companion in the world, myself, and two solitary leopards who were waiting for us in that lush paradise of color and beauty. For me, adventure doesn't get any better than that.

It really doesn't matter where one goes to find adventure in nature. It lies all around us, in our own backyards and under rocks and trees. Maybe the thing that causes me to see it easily is because I really want to. It's that simple. I'm always on the lookout. I carry my camera, journal, and watercolors wherever I go.

One year I was in Portland, Oregon, at a Women of Faith conference, and outside my hotel window was majestic Mount Hood. I saw it with early morning light, midday light, and when the evening shadows were long across it. Every minute of the day it was beautiful. I took out my watercolors and painted it in my journal—just to snatch that moment for a later recollection.

When I lived in the desert, I quite often saw road runners. They are fascinating to watch. Once I saw one in the backyard with a small frog in its mouth. It hustled up my grapefruit tree and sat on one of the branches eating the frog and tormenting two mockingbirds that wanted either the frog or the road runner. I took a snapshot. Why not? I don't have to be in Africa to see the beauty of this world. I just open my blinds and voilá! It's there. It won't ever look that way again.

As Hermann Hesse writes in his novel *Klingsor's Last Summer:*

This day will never come again and anyone who fails to eat and drink and taste and smell it will never have it offered to him again in all eternity. The sun will never shine as it does today . . . But you must play your part and sing a song, one of your best.[5]

Whether adventure takes us to our own backyard or to a distant continent, the spirit of adventure is all about staying on the lookout—keeping our eyes and our hearts open and participating fully in the moment we've been given as a pure gift. We have a part to play, a song to sing. Each experience life serves up is an opportunity to savor a moment we will never taste again. I, for one, don't want to miss a morsel.

Who are the people in your life who enrich you
and make you feel safe and happy?

_____

_____

_____

_____

_____

_____

_____

_____

_____

_____

_____

_____

_____

_____

the ledger, even
n" (all Homo Sapians) are born DEAD (I
an is born dead,
Holy God, who ca
alty of sin is d
Christ "bought us
he Cross, & the m
"made alive," Spir
teousness which is
Rom. 3:23) or, as we say

A safari is the greatest adventure in the world—whether it's in Africa or in the deepest part of your heart. Unexplored landscapes beckon.

_____

_____

_____

_____

_____

_____

_____

_____

_____

_____

_____

_____

_____

_____

_____

Life is full of serendipity. We often plan one thing and, on the way,
experience another that's even more interesting, meaningful, or unusual.
Describe a time when this happened to you.

_____

_____

_____

_____

_____

_____

_____

_____

_____

_____

_____

_____

_____

_____

_____

_____

_____

_____

_____

_____

It really doesn't matter where one goes to find adventure in nature.
It lies all around us, in our own backyards and under rocks and trees.
Maybe the thing that causes us to see it easily is that we want to.

_____

_____

_____

_____

_____

_____

_____

_____

_____

_____

_____

_____

_____

_____

_____

_____

CHAPTER SIX *Everywhere*

During a Women of Faith conference in Denver one year, a tiny mouse got on The Porch (where the speakers sit). Who knows how it got there? Perhaps it was fond of worship music and wanted to enjoy our singing up close and personal. I wish you could have seen the reaction of my porch pals when that little mouse showed up. Thelma shrieked, stuck her legs straight out in front of her and hid behind her purple purse the size of Kansas; Patsy sat on both legs until they disappeared; Sheila screamed bloody murder but didn't have to levitate since she spends her life on four-inch heels anyway; and Marilyn looked at the thing, kicked it aside, and turned to me with, "I'll bet that mouse is scared to death of all these women."

I chided the whole bunch with a characteristically loving comment: "Roaches in Africa are bigger than this little varmint. Get a grip." And we all went right back to singing "All Things Are Possible." (Fortunately, none of the eighteen thousand women in the audience knew what was happening or it wouldn't have been "The Mouse That Roared.")

In life, we have no way of knowing what's going to happen next. And, we never know for sure how we'll respond. We often plan one thing and, on the way, experience another that's even more interesting, meaningful, or unusual. Our journeys through life are regularly interrupted by detours from the intended course. On an average day, who can predict what might happen? A friend stops by with staggering news. An uninvited mouse unexpectedly scurries across our path. We win a trip to Bora Bora. What do we do now?

Several years ago Marilyn Meberg and I spoke on Mackinac Island, off the coast of the Michigan mainland. We got stranded due to bad weather. In order to catch our plane on time, we had to take a horse and buggy, boat, taxi, and bus. Literally! At every juncture it seemed one more thing went wrong. We might have worried ourselves into a very bad mood or complained and made our displeasure known to all who crossed our path. We could have had a miserable day. We certainly had all the ingredients to make us out of sorts. But we were together; and there was absolutely nothing we could do to improve our lot in life, for that day anyway. So we decided to make the most of the adventure. Having made such a good decision as that, we had the time of our lives. We've looked back on that day as one of the most memorable times of spontaneous fun we've ever enjoyed in our long friendship.

All along the way during that very unpredictable day, we played a ridiculous game. "Hey, Mare," I said, "they say we'll miss the boat because of the fog, but I don't think we will. I'll buy you breakfast if we do." She came back with a snappy retort: "You little optimist. Of course we'll miss the boat. If we don't, breakfast is on me." She bought breakfast.

Later it was obvious the taxi would not be waiting in the designated spot. "Hey, Mare," I said, "they say we'll arrive too late to catch the bus, but I don't think we will. I'll buy you lunch if we do." Marilyn responded, "You silly girl. Of course we're going to miss the bus. Look at your watch. If we don't, lunch is on me." She bought lunch.

And so the day went just like that. We were in a pickle for sure. But somehow our experience was delightful. In the end we got home without a hitch. I was very full and Marilyn, very poor. She'd picked up the tab for all three meals and every snack. Actually, it was very cheap entertainment for us both. And we laughed ourselves silly.

It's all in the attitude. Once we learn to capture these unexpected moments of surprise and potential disappointment, an even greater spirit of adventure is born in our hearts.

During a trip to visit my dear friend Sophia Stylianidou in Athens, I rented a little Volkswagen so we could poke around the Greek countryside seeing sights that were off the beaten track. Sophia knows Greece like the back of her hand, so with her as a guide, we set out one morning for Delphi. It was summer 1972. I was excited about seeing Delphi, a place I had studied in college and longed to experience for myself. Delphi, "the womb," is sacred to the Greeks. In fact, there's a stone among the ruins marked *omphalos*, or "navel" of the earth. In Greek mythology, it was here that Apollo spoke through his oracle to man; here throbbed the political intelligence center of the ancient world. In the distance, one can see Mount Parnassus, the place folks say is haunted by mythological muses. We drove along, thrilled by the prospect of this auspicious expedition.

On the way, we decided to drive off the road where we saw some workers in a field. There were men, women, and children. It looked like a photo op to me. I thought it would be a fun experience to take pictures of them at work, meet them, and have the children pose with Sophia. Eagerly, we slowed down and innocently approached them in our little car. I parked on the shoulder, and Sophia asked in Greek if I could take their picture.

Quickly, they stopped their work and gathered round the VW, and I snapped a couple of photos. All of a sudden, without warning, several of them got in the car. Others began to open our purses in the backseat and remove the contents. That was when Sophia realized these were not farm workers at all. They were gypsies, and we were in a very dangerous predicament. I was taken completely off guard and motioned a sort of "What do we do now?" sign to Sophia as she jumped into the backseat and yelled for me to just get in and "Drive!" When I finally managed to get behind the wheel, the whole gang tried to turn the car over. They rocked it from side to side as one of the women grabbed my arm and tried to remove my watch. I started the engine and sped away, dragging two men alongside the car because they refused to let go of the door handle. I was scared to death I might run over them, and I actually wondered if that was my only choice. It was one of the most frightening moments in my life.

Everybody finally let go of the car, and we burned rubber for miles to get out of there. Sophia was in the backseat, and I was driving. Eventually, when we knew we were safe, I stopped the car and got out. Sophia crawled out of the backseat, and we hugged each other in tears, grateful to be alive. When we got home that night, Sophia's parents asked about our seeing Delphi, and we winked at each other. The historic sights of the day paled in comparison to the hair-raising incident with the gypsies.

That kind of adventure I do not recommend. Nobody invites moments of danger into life on purpose, nor do most of us voluntarily put ourselves in harm's way. On the contrary, we try our best to avoid such possibilities. But when dangerous situations come our way, they teach us something about ourselves and strengthen us for times in the future when we're confronted with the unforeseeable. Unique experiences such as the one with the gypsies test our mettle to handle both adversity and the inevitable unpredictability of life.

I had a similar experience in Africa. Our trusted American travel agent, on whom we've relied for years to provide us with absolutely safe and decidedly outstanding foreign adventures, arranged for a Kenyan national named Brown to drive us from Nairobi to Samburu, about a four-hour journey. I had been told that this particular road was well-known for bandits, but that the local police had cleaned up the area and it was now safe to go by car. I got that information straight from Josephine, the travel agent; she's never been wrong. With that in mind, and since most of our travel was by air, I suggested the car trip so we could see a little of the countryside.

No problem on the way there. We had a lovely time in Samburu at Larson's Tented Camp, and we were scheduled to return to Nairobi by way of a little town called Isiolo, a tiny dot of a place about twenty-five miles south of Samburu. The road on the way is full of potholes, deep dips, boulders, gravel, and ruts. The van in which we were riding felt as if we were inside a washing machine or sliding down a washboard. I had bruises all over at the end of that hair-raising trip.

As we drove along, I asked Brown if there were many accidents on that lousy road, and he said, "Luci, I will tell you later." Hmmm. Now that piqued my interest. The car got very quiet. We traveled in absolute silence for about an hour. Then Brown, in a very steady voice, broke the stillness. "I can tell you now," he said calmly, and he proceeded to share with us a spine-tingling story while we sat in rapt attention: "Four or five years ago a friend and I were transporting two vanloads of tourists on this very road. My friend was ahead of me by a few kilometers, when his car went down into one of these dips and never came up. I slowed down and waited, wondering what had happened to him. When I finally went into the dip myself, I saw that my friend had been killed. The passengers were standing there in the road, and the van with all the luggage had been stolen."

We were stunned. Not only stunned, but horrified. Had we not just taken our lives into our own hands? Were we crazy? But we had no way of knowing. When we pulled into Isiolo and stopped for gas at a service station, the place was swarming with hawkers selling their wares. As Brown pumped the gas, they stood outside our van staring at us, trying to reach our purses, jewelry, and cameras. We all decided we didn't need to get out of the van. Four women, and not a single one of us needed to go to the bathroom, get a drink, or shop for treasures? Nope. Not us. We were perfectly content just to sit in that hot vehicle with every door locked and every window sealed shut.

As we drove into Nairobi that evening after dark, Brown cautioned us to be sure our windows and doors were still locked. It's a good thing. Just as we entered a roundabout crowded with pedestrians, a man walking in the road banged on the right side of the car door with his fist as a second man tried to open the door on the left. They were in cahoots and had seen inside the van exactly what they wanted. Fortunately, we had followed Brown's injunction to lock up and were perfectly safe. A bit breathless, but safe.

Life is full of serendipitous and surprising detours—not all of them easily accepted at the moment. We've all experienced life taking sudden turns. Sometimes we're carefree tourists and find ourselves in risky positions. Usually we're minding our own business, and quite suddenly, we encounter the unexpected. These things happen in our lives every day, and we have the choice to either embrace our experience with a sense of trust or spend our energies fighting the inevitable. We can respond to challenges and opportunities with "Why not?" or we can react to reality with "Why me?" It is truly up to us how we'll encounter what is around the next bend.

Some time ago, I broke my leg. Helping a friend trim back a large fern on her patio, I slipped and fell. The fibula bone in my left leg snapped in a six-inch-long break. I was rushed to the hospital for immediate surgery, and in order for the healing process to begin, the orthopedic surgeon put seven screws into that small bone, attaching it to the tibia, the larger bone next to it.

Since the break was so serious, I could envision my whole life stopping for a period of time. It was indeed a classic opportunity for me to determine how I would deal with formidable obstacles. I could feel defeated, put my schedule on hold, stop traveling, and mope around—all of which were tempting. Or . . . I could turn this time of healing into an adventure. The choice was mine and mine alone.

After a bit of soul-searching and carefully looking over the busy schedule that stretched out for several months in front of me, I decided to bite the bullet and go for the latter. I determined to do whatever it took to keep my spirits up. I took God at his word—that he would be with me and take care of me; that he'd go before me and straighten out the crooked places; that he'd be my comforter, friend, and great physician. Something about that choice had a rush in it for me. An edge. An excitement. Each day I couldn't wait to see what would happen! Even when I had all sorts of problems learning to walk on crutches (I even threw them across the room a couple of times), I was still glad I had chosen to live as fully as I could under the circumstances.

It was absolutely amazing the joys and surprises that were mine. Within the six months it took my leg to heal, I was in a cast, on crutches, in a wheelchair, and walking with a cane. During that time I gave dinner parties, spoke fifteen times at meetings (nine of which were in other states), went to work each day, and drove my car all over the place. I went on vacation in Colorado, and—the pièce de résistance—I traveled to Paris with friends and to Italy for a wedding. Never once did I regret my choices. My adventures took me everywhere. In spite of the hardships, I had wonderful, unforgettable times that are etched in my memory forever.

When we trust God outside of our comfort zones, anything can happen, anywhere. And sometimes what happens is utterly delightful.

I certainly was not prepared for what happened to me in Ghana, West

Africa, a few years ago. It gives me a deep chuckle each time I think about it. I was on a mission trip with World Vision, the relief organization that does so much for people in developing countries. Women of Faith had been invited to participate in one of their projects, and I had the happy privilege of being included in the traveling troupe.

One afternoon we were all invited to a durbar, a large assembly where numerous African groups and tribes come together dressed in the full regalia of their culture. There must have been three thousand people in all—men, women, and children. There was a program, music, traditional dancing, and addresses given by different persons (including some of us from the States). The festivities lasted three hours in the searing heat of the summer sun. We Americans were all perspiring excessively and fanning ourselves, while the nationals sat around in heavy garb, cool as cucumbers. Amazing to watch! At their request, Thelma Wells and I sang and spoke. Not understanding a word of English did not keep our audience from giving us thunderous applause.

My newest Adventure —
a broken leg

I hadn't been there long when the chairperson walked over to me and whispered in my ear, "The Ghanaian queen mother would like to dance with you." I smiled at the gentleman and took a few seconds to comprehend what he had said. Then I wondered what he meant. I knew I didn't want to offend the queen by refusing to dance, although the idea sounded strange to me at first.

It became obvious, however, that the queen mother was accustomed to getting what she wanted. It hardly mattered that I wondered if I'd look funny dancing with the queen. So, self-consciousness aside, I got up from my chair, walked out onto that dusty field, bowed to the queen mother, and together we danced to the beat of those wild, wonderful African drums! It didn't take me long to get into the spirit of the affair. It was delightful! The crowd was wildly enthusiastic. Either we were fabulous, or they were well aware of how to respond to the queen mother's performance. I held nothing back, and neither did she. Here we were: one white, one black; one young, one old (ahem! I was the young one); one American, one African; one single, one married; one in jeans, the other in finery; two women, dancing together for all the world to see and enjoy. I'll tell you, if that wasn't a memory to cherish, I don't know what was. Afterward, we laughed and hugged and thanked each other, then returned to our seats with the audience still applauding.

Would that we could always have this kind of curiosity and verve about life, saying "yes!" to its strange and unusual possibilities. God gave us life and vitality and a sense of wonder, and an enormous capacity to flourish emotionally, personally, and spiritually. Why do we often hold back? Why do we wait? Why are we afraid? Why not live fully and completely—regardless of the circumstances we encounter? Why not do life differently?

The most interesting people I know drink in life and savor every drop—the sweet and the sour. The good and the bad. The planned and the unplanned. And isn't that what God intends? When Jesus modeled humanity for you and me to see, he was out there—everywhere! He took risks. He embraced life and responded to everyone and everything, the tender and the tumultuous. His capacity for life was without measure. And we are designed like him. Fully human and fully alive. I don't want to miss anything he has in store for me, even if the path he takes me on winds through some pretty rough terrain. Right in the midst of what seems to me to be a detour from the map, I'm often gifted with something precious and unforgettable.

Capturing the moment is a choice, a way of life. It requires us to wake up, live life, and be present—here, there, and everywhere. Sometimes that's scary; sometimes it's exhilarating. Always it's an adventure I keep learning to welcome with a full and grateful heart.

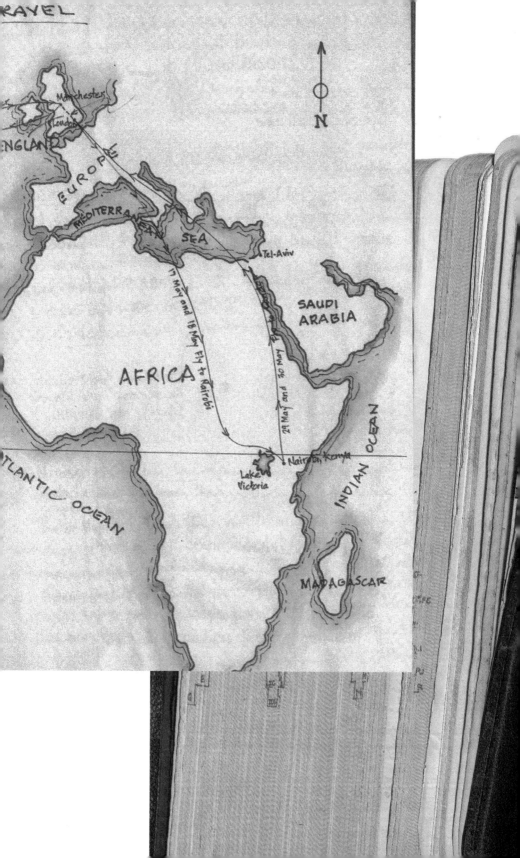

Make a graph on which you chart your life's journey.

_____

_____

_____

_____

_____

_____

_____

_____

_____

_____

_____

_____

_____

_____

Plot Your Lifeline

Drawing your lifeline involves viewing your life in terms of your successes and failures, highs and lows, and plotting the results as a graph. As you can see in the example here, age increases along the X-axis and relative success or failure along the Y-axis.

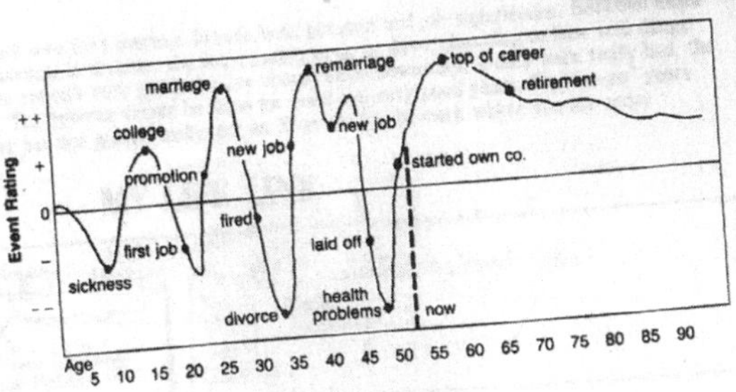

From: THE EXECUTIVE FEMALE Magazine
January/February 1986 pg. 31-34

An upright man gives thought to his ways.

—*Proverbs 21:29*

_____

_____

_____

_____

_____

_____

_____

_____

_____

_____

_____

_____

_____

_____

_____

_____

Never say "never." You have no idea when you might have to eat that word. Life is crammed with possibilities just on the other side of "never."

"The very things I hated became the making of me."

How true is that for you?

PART 3

CAPTURING THE LIGHT

PART 3

About twenty-five years before the golden decade of French Impressionism, a British painter named Joseph Mallord William Turner achieved something nobody ever had before. I would kill to own one of his paintings. Don't worry. None of them is available, and I couldn't afford one anyway.

Most Turner paintings are housed at the Tate Gallery in London in a building called the Clore Gallery. It is highly unusual for an artist to have his own gallery, but because of Turner's importance and achievements, he does. The seventy-five-plus years of Turner's life (1775–1851) were a very exciting period in art history. Creative output during the romantic movement was prodigious. Great musical compositions, novels, poems, and paintings of that period are still popular today. Composers, poets, authors, and painters of that day considered themselves to be unique individuals. They loved new experiences and felt their imagination should be given freedom to explore the unknown. They took risks.

This was Turner! He was an adventurer and a loner who never married, was passionate about life, loved to travel, thrived on figuring things out, and always embraced an element of danger. We are very much alike in many of those things. Maybe that's why I admire him so. I see myself in some of his pursuits.

But the impact he had on modern painting is without parallel. Turner was the first artist to figure out that color could speak to us independent of subject matter or form. In a sense, he liberated color from being simply a tool for the artist and gave it a life of its own. And the best gift he gave all of us who have the joy of seeing his work is that of capturing light. Standing before his paintings gives one the feeling of being surrounded by virtual luminescence—as if a ray of sunlight coming from inside the painting has fallen on you.

I've tried to figure this out, to understand what it is that Turner did when he painted a scene or seascape, and the only way I can describe it is to say it's like looking at the sun through a mirage. Something is there, but it's not. I see it, but I don't. I make out a form but not really. A lot is left to my imagination, yet it is so well done that I never quite get enough. There is a delicate, soft, ethereal force that keeps drawing me back.

I vividly recall a time in 1995 when I stood in the National Gallery in London, eager to see the special exhibit featuring one of Turner's paintings. Only one: *The Fighting Temeraire.* Some scholars consider this painting a "thoroughly perfect picture." The *Temeraire* was a man-of-war that had fought heroically at the Battle of Trafalgar. But in Turner's painting it is being towed by a steam tug to be broken up. The famous ship and tiny black tugboat are on the left side in the painting, and a great light is on the right—way off in the distance.

Turner spent most of his boyhood around boats and ships, and he loved the sea. He actually witnessed this very tugboat pulling the *Temeraire* to shore in 1838 and decided it was a good subject to paint. But what captivated me was the light in the distance, not the ship or the tugboat or the fact that all the fighting days were over.

If the painting could speak, it would say to me, "There is still magic in the world, Luci. It's in the light . . . in the distance. Look for the light. Don't fret over what's been lost or what has to be replaced or what is damaged and being dragged to shore—concentrate on the light." More than any other artist, Turner's work reminds me that even though I may not be able to explain it to anybody else or sometimes even to myself, the strength I need is in the light, in the sublime, although it may appear as only a mirage. When I look at this artist's work, I think of John 9:5 where Jesus says, "I am the light of the world." Keeping my eyes on Jesus, I can do anything. I can walk in light even on my darkest days.

Living in the light is one of the most difficult tasks we have. It means getting out of the way so there is no shadow blocking the source. When we read or write or engage in hobbies or reach out to others, why do we do that? What do we hope to gain? I think it's to be illuminated—enlightened—or we hope to give off illumination of some kind. That's what light is: illumination—whether emotional, financial, mental, physical, or spiritual.

To capture the light available to us is one more aspect of divining the spirit of adventure. The more light we live in, the more we grow and change.

Every day God reminds us to quit holding things too tightly—whether an event, a viewpoint, a desire, a particular time in life, or a person we thoroughly enjoy. He urges us to stop struggling, resisting, coercing, or manipulating for what we want. When we simply do what he asks, no matter how hard it seems, and we keep our focus on the Light of the World, an amazing brightness comes, all within the embrace of his love.

> Man's life is a day. What is he?
> What is he not? A shadow in a dream
> Is man: but when God sheds a brightness,
> Shining light is on earth
> And life is sweet as honey.[6]

In the formative years of my childhood, my parents were the human factors that provided the nourishment I needed to begin growing. They put me on a playing field where the game of life began. With their teachings as a springboard, I started making decisions that caused me to be the person I am today, for good or bad.

As I branched out and began seeing patterns form, traveling revealed an adventuresome side of my temperament. I went here, did this, saw that, and felt thus and so. My friend Mary says, "People do what makes sense to them," and it's true. We all have to determine what makes sense to us and do it, whether or not it seems logical to anyone else. We don't live fully until we do this for ourselves. Some of the things that make sense to me are art, music, photography, literature, and theater. These are the considerations in life that turn my crank, make me think, and fill my heart with appreciation and wonder. They are vehicles that transport me into the light that illuminates and enriches my journey.

ART

The field of art is open to the whole world. It exists inside every human being. You don't have to be able to draw or paint to be an artist. You have to search, feel, and dare to express yourself. I've always known this intuitively, but getting my bachelor's degree in art really helped me to look at life in a different way, to recognize that the human brain can be a kaleidoscopic lens. It opens a shutter to appreciating, savoring, and seeing beauty around me. Viewing life in this way enriches my soul and becomes a path toward wholeness and authenticity.

When I look at paintings or sculpture, I often see more than what is right in front of me. For example, I have on my desk a copy of a small piece of sculpture I saw in the Museum of Cycladic Art in Athens, Greece. I have had this little piece for years, and it has always been in a prominent place.

Cycladic Art Figurine (on my desk)

I look at it every day. The original, carved by an artisan in the third millennium BC, is a simple white marble female figurine in a clean, severe style. Nothing about it is soft or what I would call beautiful to look at. But phere's why I love it: every time I glance at that figure, I'm reminded that everything starts simply. *Don't mess this up, Luci, by making it complex. Simple lines. Simple thoughts. Simple premise.* I often say those things to myself when I begin a project. Any project.

At times when I'm burdened by something, I look at that figure and remember, *Jesus loves me.* What's simpler than that truth? Or if I'm confused about what to do in a certain situation, I glance at the figurine, which says in effect, *Go back to the beginning of the problem and work it through . . . piece by piece by piece.* I've had writer's block, and that carving has encouraged me to calm down, simplify the story, and quit trying to say something I know nothing about. Over and over this little figurine has sent me back to the basics. Maybe this information is of no great shakes to you, but to me it's foundational to who I am. Art represents much more than what I'm looking at. It's a springboard for associative thinking.

Here's another example. Not far from where the Cycladic figure sits is a large, framed Picasso print of an original that hangs in the Tate Gallery in London. I've stood in front of the original several times and have always been moved in the same way. It's called *The Weeping Woman.* I love this strange, fascinating painting. It's a contorted, grotesque, abstract head of a woman who is crying her heart out. At the location of her saucer-shaped eyes are tiny, capsized boats, out of which looping tears run down her face. Her knotted green hands are holding a white handkerchief, pressed up to her anguished eyes. Everything about that face speaks of sorrow and grief. There are even black vultures reflected in each eye, saying to the viewer that she is being eaten alive with pain. One might wonder why she is well

"The Weeping Woman" by Pablo Picasso

dressed, wearing a red hat with a blue flower on it, yet so disheveled and contorted underneath. The two seem incongruous.

Why would I have that weird painting on my wall? Because I have cried that deeply. So much so I thought my heart would break. Even though I might have been dressed in nice clothes and looked "together" on the outside, I was torn apart inside, thinking I would die from the heartache. The tears wouldn't stop. They filled up little imaginary boats until the boats tilted over and drenched my cheeks.

When I'm that broken, there is one who will meet me in my pain—the Lord Jesus. Scripture says he is acquainted with our sorrow. "His heart is touched" with my grief, it says. If I can be that broken and he can be that touched, then knowing him is an enormous respite to my soul. This painting captures private moments in my life I might never be able to share with another human being because they are so disconcerting to witness. But right square in the middle of the dichotomy of looking as if I have it together when I'm really falling apart, God is there too. He understands my heart.

The Creator of all loves me. He notices every detail of my personal land-scape; he sees with an artist's eye. An artist is simply one who looks at life. He or she is interested and interesting. When we're interested, we ask our-selves questions about life. We're curious about our own inner world. We wonder. Ponder. Hunt. We study what is in front of us and look deeper than the outside form. We see beyond the obvious and have a greater sense of truth and meaning than we do when we fail to really see. We experience illu-mination, enlightenment, personal and spiritual growth.

One artist who has influenced my thinking along these lines is Robert Henri, a painter whose realistic paintings caught slices of everyday life in action—back alleys, street scenes, laundry hanging on the line, working people. I've seen Henri's paintings in numerous museums and like them well enough, but the reason I love Robert Henri has little to do with his paintings. My love is based on a book he wrote way back in 1923, seven years before his death, called *The Art Spirit*. In it he sought to tell his students how to look at life. My little paperback copy is dog-eared and dingy because I refer to it all the time for encouragement and remembrance of what mat-ters. The opening paragraph reads:

> There are moments in our lives, there are moments in a day, when we seem to see beyond the usual. Such are the moments of our greatest happiness. Such are the moments of our greatest wisdom. If one could but recall his vision by some sort of sign. It was in this hope that the arts were invented. Sign-posts on the way to what may be. Sign-posts toward greater knowledge.[7]

This is what I mean by capturing the light. Enlightened moments pro-vide our greatest happiness or greatest wisdom. They are "sign-posts toward greater knowledge"—and, I believe, richer experiences of the living God in whose image we are created.

The Art Spirit is my favorite book on the subject of art because it's all about art relating to life. Another book that had a profound influence on my life is *The Power of Art* by John Warbeke. I bought it at a garage sale for a buck, and the information in it is worth thousands to me now. I read it through the same year as *The Art Spirit* and found it to be a valuable source related to the quality of life I want to live. What it taught me gave character to my somewhat average environment. It encompasses so much of what I love—painting, sculpture, music, poetry, theater, architecture—all the products of civilization. And it appeals to the side of me that longs to find meaning in everything—my spiritual beliefs, relationships, work, all of life's experiences. I underlined everything that mattered and copied it into a big journal that I carried around and studied. I meant business with that thing! I was determined that my life wouldn't be dull or boring, and I wanted to know anything that would add quality to everything I did or thought. I found a lot of that in *The Power of Art*. It was the vehicle I rode into larger vistas.

My whole point in this treatise about art is that each of us has the whole creation as our oyster. We can make our own choices as to what we like and dislike. But before we claim that "right," we must know a little bit. The more we know, the more fun we have exploring both the spirit of art within and the progeny of creation all around us. So go ahead: expose yourself to the light around you, opening the closed doors and windows inside your soul. You don't have to go to a class to get that education. You can do it on your own. Read art critiques in the newspaper, go to museums, take notes, form your own opinions. In short, think for yourself and decide what you think and feel based upon your own viewpoint and experience.

Art is so much fun. There is nothing to be put off by except our own fear that we're not smart enough to understand it. But . . . we are. We are the recipients of centuries of beauty and bounty that can feed our souls for the whole of our lives if we just open the door.

PHOTOGRAPHY

When I sat down to work on this chapter, I could not turn on my computer. It simply wouldn't start. I hate it when that happens. (I named the computer the *Moonship*, because I was sure it went through orbits somewhere in the middle of the night when I wasn't looking. Lots of buttons, bells, and whistles. The family genius, Orville, built it for me. It could do anything. Probably even cook up an omelet.)

I punched the start button twice and nothing happened. So I turned my eyes toward heaven and said, "Lord, am I gonna have to shoot this thing?" punched it again, and it started right up. I'm so glad God hears my prayers.

This is the way I feel sometimes about camera equipment. I've had all kinds of trouble. Anything mechanical has that built-in possibility. I bought a tripod once to take on my first trip to Africa, and before I got out of the driveway, my backpack fell over with the tripod attached, and the entire camera platform broke off. I kept thinking I'd fix it somewhere along the way (never did) and lugged it around for two weeks in the Serengeti bush. So I know how it feels when something doesn't work and you're stuck with it. Yet in spite of potential mechanical problems, It has never kept me from collecting camera equipment. I love having a good camera and everything that goes with it.

The first question a photographer has to answer is, "What is my goal?" If you want to capture Sunday afternoon in the park with your family or a few photos at the beach and have no other motive than to make prints and pass them around, then it's not important that you know a great deal about cameras, buy the most expensive equipment, or invest a lot of time in this hobby. Point, shoot, have fun, and you've got it! If, on the other hand, your ambition is to be a great photographer, then having the proper equipment is essential.

Nothing, however, is more important than developing a good eye. While some photographers have an innate ability to take superb pictures, most of us are simply doing our best to focus on a subject, remember the cumulative knowledge we've learned through the years, and snap the picture at the right time. Volumes have been written on the discipline of photography, and I have fifteen or sixteen books in my own collection. But all the reading and studying in the world won't help me take great pictures if I don't develop my "eye" and try to understand why I want the picture in the first place.

There is something about practicing photography that refines my vision.

It forces me to focus on what's important and causes all the peripheral stuff to drop away. As I patiently wait for the light to fall on my subject, I'm constantly thinking of how to capture that moment in its best illumination. I don't care if you have a Brownie Reflex, a point-and-shoot homemade camera, or the latest fancy digital, you still need a refined eye that knows what it wants and goes after it purposefully. The outcome is full of possibilities, but I can guarantee you this: When we let our critical eye dictate the setting for the shot, we are more likely to end up with the photo we want and create a wonderful memory as well.

One Halloween I carved the face of a cat in a pumpkin, and when I lit a candle inside, it looked exactly like a cat. Unbelievable, Lucille. You're a genius! I was dying to get a picture of it because I didn't ever want to forget the work that went into that little piece of sculpture. I would need a tripod to hold the camera steady long enough to get the shot. I lit the candle, set the pumpkin on the counter in my kitchen, attached my camera to the tripod, put the setting on ambient light (no flash), and took a whole roll of shots. Nearly all of them were good. I yelled! The carving was a wonderful adventure and the evening so enjoyable. The photo captured a fun and fulfilling moment for me that I'll

never forget. I can't even look at it now without smiling. It is cradled in my memory bank so I can lovingly embrace it whenever and wherever I am. Anybody want a cat picture? Everyone got a copy in his or her Christmas card that year. Merry Halloween.

cat-carved in a pumpkin.

When I don't have opportunity to set up the tripod, I go with what's at hand. In the fall of 1997, I took one of my best shots ever by propping my zoom lens on somebody's shoulder in front of me. I was at the Kennedy Space Center in Florida taking night pictures of the *Atlantis* liftoff. A group of us was seated in bleachers about three miles away, but we could see the whole thing. I took three rolls of film and got one shot that was especially good. In fact . . . it was incredible! The timing was perfect—a split second

'Atlantis' liftoff...1997.

after liftoff (10:37 p.m.). Smoke is billowing up all around the tower, the space capsule is lifting off the earth into the night sky, and everything is as clear as a bell. Because I'm an amateur, that shot alone gives me courage to keep trying to capture my life on film.

Numerous places on earth are a photographer's dream. When I took photos of the Taj Mahal, for example, I was transferring poetry to film. One could take pictures of that marvelous building all day and never tire of a new way of seeing it. African safaris offer countless photo opportunities. Even rush hour in New York City has a beauty all its own. As did my tiny patio garden outside my small condo in the Southern California desert. There's no end to what the world offers in the grand and glorious field of photography. I want to develop a better eye to see the light God brings into my pathway, and I hope I have my camera in hand when that happens.

LITERATURE

You know how certain authors appear on the horizon of your life, and you want to read everything they've written? What they have to say and how they say it not only influences your thoughts but also validates what you were already pondering. That was my case in the early seventies when I discovered the writings of Hermann Hesse. In the 1920s and 1930s, Hesse had a following of students who took his novels as an invitation to pour out their hearts to him. He received hundreds of letters asking for advice. Unwittingly, he became their father confessor. I never felt this way about him, but I did read everything he wrote and was strangely moved by his thoughts and lucid descriptions.

What appealed to students—rebellion against the establishment, quest for personal values, metaphysical contemplations—was not what appealed to me. And the odd thing is I'm not much of a fiction fan, yet I could not stop reading Hesse until I exhausted the whole collection. Rather than making me want to rebel against acceptable society, his books gave me an inexplicable peace. Rather than uprooting or altering my own value system, they assured me I was right about what I believed. Rather than encouraging me to investigate the metaphysical universe, they drove me more into God's truth as revealed in Scripture. I was Hesse's avid student for more than twenty years, for entirely different reasons than his usual followers.

First of all, almost every character in Hesse's novels demonstrates an observable dichotomy. They could be warm and cold, happy and sad, detached and involved, not wanting to do something but doing it anyway. They often had trouble coming to terms with themselves. I recognized myself. As I read, I saw that I wanted to do things but didn't, take part but held back, felt okay about being me but didn't, did dumb things then wondered why. In Romans 7 the apostle Paul talks about not understanding himself . . . deciding to do something then doing the opposite. Why? Because he was dealing with the dichotomy within himself. I recognized these patterns in myself as I read page after page of Hesse. It was as if I were reading my own diary.

One of Hesse's greatest themes is that everything is transitory. It will be here today but fly away tomorrow with the wind. His writings encouraged me to live fully every moment. I knew intuitively how important this is to experiencing the adventure of life, but Hesse captured my own philosophy in poignant prose. By the time I became acquainted with his writings, I had already lost good friends very suddenly in death, so I had reason to think about the fragility of life.

I used to think that life would get better. If I planned it right—worked harder, denied myself, saved more money, figured it all out—one day I'd wake up and everything would be okay, or at least better. What Hesse helped me see is that it doesn't get any better than this, because the "this" of life is what I make it, not what happens outside myself. If I don't live fully in the moment, there's no rewinding or playing forward that assures me of a better day. A little neon light went on in my brain that kept blinking, *This is it, Lucille. Live with all your heart today because life is transitory, and it doesn't get any better. The "better" of life is now.* That helped me enormously with my attitude. When I would forget and regress, I'd just switch on the neon light in my brain and remember, *This is it.* I still do that often.

My very favorite aspect of Hermann Hesse's work is that he reminds us that everything in life has an opposite. If one experiences happiness, he's able to do that because he has known sadness. If he experiences good health, he enjoys it more having known sickness. In other words, every zenith has a nadir. And the ability to feel anything is based on the degree to which we experience its opposite. In fact, one can't live a life of feeling very much of anything without knowing both ends of the spectrum. Having both in a life is what builds character and keeps it from being flat, average, or boring.

When this truth became part of my life, I began to understand the value of good and bad, easy and hard, light and darkness. I remembered a word I learned in a college art history class—*chiaroscuro.* I knew what it meant in painting but had no idea it applied to life.

Chiaroscuro comes from two Italian words: *chiaro*, which means clear or light, and *oscuro*, which means dark. In painting they refer to a pictorial representation in terms of light and shadow. In Hessian characters, there is always chiaroscuro. That's why they're interesting. They have clarity and obscurity. They're like us. Much about human nature is understandable—forthright and clear—but there are things we'll never understand, no matter how well we get to know ourselves. How often have you thought, *Why in the world did I do that? That's not like me.* We do it because we're human, and humanity is an enigma unto itself.

Hermann Hesse helps me understand, tolerate, and accept human reality and its limitations. Even in myself. I don't have to be superwoman, leaping over tall buildings to rescue someone in need. I can just be me, with my own frailties and problems and yearnings and needs—and it's okay. There will always be the tension—the light and dark—between my mind and spirit. As is true of all good literature, the writings of this prolific author give me a better understanding of my spiritual nature. He gives me the perspective to view the urgencies and conflicts of life more calmly and rationally.

You may be saying, "Who cares about all this stuff, Luci?" Maybe nobody but me. But I believe these truths are vitally important to anyone who tries to understand his or her life and embrace it as an adventure. When we know, to the degree we are able, what we think and why we think it, we experience more richness in life. The truth is there all the time, but it's the knowing it and understanding it that makes it our own.

I love books and could talk books for days. I could also write an entire volume on the books that have pushed me forward, helped me grow, turned me around from the direction I was heading, or simply given me hours of great pleasure. I chose to write about Hesse because he has brought so much personal clarity into my life. From the illumination of his words, I dared to be myself and keep dreaming my dreams. He picked up my soul in a time of need and helped me live life in a different way.

THEATER

When I first moved to California from Texas thirty years ago, I got season tickets to the famous Huntington Hartford Theater in Hollywood and went with Marilyn Meberg to a Saturday matinee each month. The anticipation of going was a great part of the thrill, but afterward we were even more excited and gratified for having spent our time that way. The plays we saw always evoked the most scintillating discussions about life, love, death, betrayal, humor, struggle, friendship, patriotism—all the feelings of real life.

Marilyn is a nut for theater, a wonderful listener, and unparalleled in asking thought-provoking questions. It was as though we were transported to another planet on those wild and unforgettable forays. I've often thought back on the plays we saw, remembering some of the things we learned about each other, people in general, society, and civilization.

Drama may be the greatest catalytic force in the world because it holds a mirror up to human actions and motivations. We see ourselves in our most comprehensive temperaments—strong and weak, wise and foolish, delightful and painful, tragic and comedic.

Consider a play that proves my point: *The Price* by Arthur Miller. It has four characters: Victor and Esther Franz (husband and wife), Walter Franz (brother to Victor), and Gregory Solomon (a furniture dealer). Briefly, the plot revolves around these two estranged brothers trying to dispose of their deceased parents' property and the confrontations that ensue, leading them to examine the events of their own lives and attitudes toward existence. Walter is a surgeon, and Victor, a policeman. Because of their diverse professions and the duplicity of their father toward each son, there have been unresolved conflicts between them for years. And now they find themselves facing the task of trying to agree upon what and how to dispose of a houseful of old furniture. The dealer, Gregory Solomon, is nothing more than a facilitator of conversation, keeping the play on course.

A fine balance of sympathy is evoked for both Victor and Walter. The more open and vulnerable each man is, the more the viewer is inclined to feel the actor's pain and be sympathetic. The more closed, the more quickly we judge. This balance is what makes the play a masterpiece. In the end, each of the brothers' viewpoints simply prove what the other already knew about himself but dared not face until the moment was forced upon him.

Life is like this. When I'm vulnerable enough to present myself to another in my humanity, it evokes empathy; but when I put on a front and hide the real me, it becomes a sham and makes for misunderstandings. This delicate balance of being honest yet not foolishly transparent is very difficult but something toward which I constantly strive, because I believe it is the best way to live. The most honest way. As I grow older, much of what I am (or was) is simply forfeited to the passing of time. But as more of the real me is left, I am able to touch the true structure and fabric of who I am and why it is important to be myself. If I'm honest with myself, I'm then capable of being honest with everybody else. In the words of Shakespeare:

> This above all: to thine own self be true,
> And it must follow, as the night the day,
> Thou canst not then be false to any man.[8]

The Price is about sacrifice, choices, openness, honesty, loyalty, and moral dilemmas. During the first half of the play, one has the illusion the story is about negotiating a good fee for a pile of old furniture, when in fact it is about the price we pay to live authentically. This is an issue we face every day. Can I answer this question: How willing am I to be totally myself, and what will it cost me? That is the heart of the play. It makes me contemplate, and, as you know, I love contemplation.

For example, here's a bit of contemplation I had when I first saw the play: No one can escape inner conflict. Unfortunately, it's a major part of daily living. Even those two brothers had not realized the dilemma each faced in his own heart until he was confronted with his true self—or better put, his true selfishness. Each had to pay the price of admitting who he was inside in order to have a real life. How embarrassing—yet how life changing. This "price" was the making of those men. It's like poet Robert Browning's line "When the fight begins within himself, a man is worth something."

So the heart of the play has a spiritual point: when we realize our inner struggle has value and that God is using it to change us to be more like him, we're liberated to grow within and actually change for the better. We become sweeter and stronger. And those new energies allow us to meet outside difficulties in a way that benefits others as well. Thought-provoking drama is rich fare for the soul, a reminder that life itself is art—illuminating, vast, an endless adventure.

MUSIC

Being part of a musical family was one of God's greatest gifts to our household, not to mention my own soul. As children, we used to gang around the piano before bedtime and sing together. Bubba (or Mother) would play piano, and all of us (except Daddy, who played harmonica) harmonized to campfire songs, hymns we had memorized, or little ditties that were popular during the early forties. I well remember doing that for an hour or so; then, as we were getting ready for bed, the phone would ring.

"Hi. This is Mrs. Bloodworth next door. Please don't stop singing; you're lulling my kids to sleep."

My mother would laugh and explain that her own kids needed to sleep, too, feeling proud of her musical brood. Life in the Swindoll household always included music. My grandparents were musical, my mother was a singer and pianist, my aunt played piano beautifully, and both my brothers play instruments. It never occurred to me that music was highbrow or inaccessible or unattainable, and I still believe that, strongly. Music, like art, is for the masses. It is one of the most important aspects of having a full life, and a home without music is poorer than the one without money.

In 1979 a group of friends asked me to make a list of records they should buy to start a library of classical music. I welcomed that challenge. Since I grew up listening to the classics, the Saturday afternoon opera performances from the Met, my brother sitting at the piano for hours trying to become a concert pianist, and my grandmother teaching piano, making that list was pure joy. There was only one problem—how was I to know what might sound good to me but not good to my friends?

"We buy records because we like the picture on the album cover," they admitted. "Then we get home and find we've got some piece of music that makes no sense to our ears, isn't pretty, and we wish we'd never bought it. Can you help us know what we like or what we want?"

I loved working on that little project, though it was a tall order because nobody is exactly alike in his or her tastes in the arts. I began researching music—most of which I knew from my own experience, some of which was new to me—and made a wonderful discovery. In terms of classical music, there is about a hundred-year period of history (1840–1940) that has the most pleasing, enjoyable, easy-to-listen-to music I think everybody should know and own. That may sound presumptuous, but having to start somewhere, this is a great place to start. It's like the little poetry book we had as kids, *Poems Every Child Should Know*. Nobody could tell every child what poetry they should know, but somebody along the way offered that book as what would be worth knowing. This is how I felt about my classical music list.

With that in mind, I want to suggest ten pieces that fall within that century-long time frame. If you've never owned any classical music, I suggest you begin your collection with these gems. They are all well-known, beautiful, worth hearing again and again, and inexpensive to buy. I suspect this music will open areas in your heart you never knew existed, just as it did for my friends. The capacity to love these melodies was there all the time . . . my friends just didn't know where to start listening.

One more thing—if I leave out your favorite musical composition, just add it to the list! Music is subjective, not objective. Make certain pieces your own. That's why they're great. They have lasted through the centuries because all of us have claimed them as our own.

BRAHMS: SYMPHONY NO. 3 IN F MAJOR, OP. 90 (1883)

Oh, this piece. Beautiful! It was written when Brahms was fifty. He had fallen in love with a twenty-six-year-old contralto. (Beware of the sultry tones of a contralto!) He was happy and healthy, and the symphony reflects all this. The minute you hear the famous melody you'll say, "Oh, yes . . . I know that. I just didn't know it was the Brahms's Third."

DVORÁK: SYMPHONY NO. 9 IN E MINOR, OP. 95 (1892)

All four movements of this symphony will probably be recognizable to you. Dvorak was born in Bohemia but came to America and loved Negro spirituals—all their tender, passionate, melancholy, religious themes—and this "new world" symphony speaks of his American experience.

MAHLER: SYMPHONY NO. 2 IN C MINOR, "RESURRECTION" (1894)

Out of the ten symphonies Mahler wrote, this is a knockout! I have a feeling some glorious orchestra will be playing it on our resurrection day, because it's the perfect music to rise by. There's a great, huge chorus in it (not to mention a gorgeous duet between soprano and alto) where the words speak of conquering death, to live again forever and ever. I'm trying to memorize the words to be ready to sing when Jesus returns to take us home to glory.

TCHAIKOVSKY: SYMPHONY NO. 6 IN B MINOR,
OP. 74, "PATHETIQUE" (1893)

Tchaikovsky was fifty when he wrote this, so he knew a good bit about living. The four movements deal with what we face as human beings: life, love, disappointment, and death. This beautiful, moving symphony is reflective of Tchaikovsky's life of sorrow. Ironically, a few days after it was first performed, Tchaikovsky died.

RACHMANINOFF: PIANO CONCERTO NO. 2 IN C MINOR,
OP. 18 (1901)

This popular, large-scale work is one of the most famous piano concertos in the world. You've heard it a hundred times. Some people may think it's hackneyed, but not I. To me, it outranks everything else written for piano. I'd give anything to have composed it myself. When you hear the melody to "Full Moon and Empty Arms," you'll remember it right off the bat.

GRIEG: CONCERTO FOR PIANO AND ORCHESTRA
IN A MINOR, OP. 16 (1868)

Believe it or not, Grieg wrote this piece—his only piano concerto—when he was only twenty-five. (What was I doing at that tender age?) He and his wife had just had a baby daughter, and the music reflects his happiness. It's packed with full, rich chords, sounding like a Norwegian folk song at times.

SAINT-SAËNS: CONCERTO FOR PIANO AND ORCHESTRA NO. 2 IN G MINOR, OP. 22 (1868)

Are you ready for this? Saint-Saëns was good at everything. He was a playwright, critic, essayist, composer, conductor, and pianist. At home with high society or bohemians, he was a witty clown, a crusader, a distinguished man of the world, and a composer of songs for children as well as adults. This piano concerto has it all—runs, trills, thundering chords—the works!

BRUCH: CONCERTO NO. 1 IN G MINOR FOR VIOLIN AND ORCHESTRA, OP. 26 (1868)

Although Bruch was a well-known composer and conductor, his claim to fame is this concerto. At the age of nineteen he started jotting down ideas for it and conducted it for the first time when he was twenty-six. Of all the violin concertos written, this is my favorite.

MENDELSSOHN: CONCERTO IN E MINOR FOR VIOLIN AND ORCHESTRA, OP. 64 (1844)

Written three years before Mendelssohn died, this moody, melancholy piece is a must to own! It's written in the minor key, characteristic of all pieces for solo instruments by Mendelssohn. I always think of Vincent van Gogh's paintings when I hear this composer's music. Both men died in their mid-thirties yet gave us enough beauty to last through the ages. This piece will make your heart ache and your spirit sing.

POULENC: CONCERTO FOR TWO PIANOS AND ORCHESTRA IN D MINOR (1932)

I could hardly wait to list this concerto, because I love it to pieces. It was written the year I was born and is dynamite. Very modern and full of zest. It's based on popular Parisian tunes of the day. The two pianos play tag throughout. Lots to listen to, and you're never ever bored or distracted. Oh, and somewhere in all this is the most romantic or sentimental (a better word for it) interlude that will move your heart deeply.

There you have it—ten beginning pieces to a classical library. Before you run me out of town because I listed no Beethoven, let me explain myself. I don't like Beethoven. I don't know if my taste is too bourgeois,

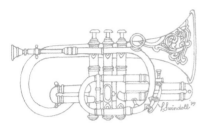

or if most of his music is just too loud. Since he wrote a good bit of it when he was deaf, I feel like the sound should be lowered before the music's turned on. I realize Beethoven was a composer of tremendous optimism, but somehow that doesn't help me like his music. If you like him, though, add him to this list and get these pieces: Symphony no. 3 in E-flat Major, op. 55, "Eroica"; Concerto in D Major for Violin and Orchestra, op. 61; and Sonata no. 7 in D Major, op. 10, no. 3. They're all lovely, rich pieces, even though they're by Beethoven. Check them out for yourself and make your own decision.

A final word—if you're on a desert island and can only take one piece of music with you, I would suggest something that will fill your heart in every single way. It's not on this list because it's not in that hundred-year period I prefer. But it is a must for every man, woman, boy, or girl to hear, own, and (hopefully someday) participate in—Handel's *Messiah*.

The *Messiah* was first performed in the mid-1700s and shows no sign of diminishing in popularity in the twenty-first century. It was written in only twenty-one days, in complete seclusion, by the hand of a musical genius, and every word is Scripture. I first sang in it as a young person with the members of my family.

Memorizing the alto part was only the beginning of the adventure. For seven years at Christmastime, Mother drove Chuck, Orville, and me to the First Methodist Church in downtown Houston for numerous rehearsals. Our conductor was a wonderful man named Walter Jenkins. He made the dead want to sing. Each of those years, we had the privilege of singing with an enormous choir the proclamation of Jesus coming to earth as a baby in a manger . . . to Handel's incredible orchestration.

Newsman Robert MacNeil describes my experience so well:

Music heard early in life lays down a rich bed of memories against which you evaluate and absorb music encountered later. Each layer adds to the richness of your musical experience; it ingrains expectations that will govern your taste for future music and perhaps change your feelings about music you already know.[9]

In one harmonious whole and grand swelling burst of harmony, I got to be part of a magnificent musical experience that is one of the sweetest memories of my life. A diapason of light and sound captured my heart and soul and changed both forever. This piece of music is the greatest oratorio ever written, and it is an unparalleled example of the blending of words and notes to bring glory to almighty God.

I am so grateful to have had parents who gave me a foundation in the fields of art, music, photography, literature, and theater. And not only has it given me something for my own soul, but it has given me something to give away—even to those who aren't interested in our faith.

Many years ago, before the wall came down in Eastern Europe, my friend Mary traveled to the Soviet Union. Her heart was to reach university students for Christ. So she and a few comrades made recurring trips to what was then Leningrad for this exciting mission. On her first trip she met four students, all English majors at Leningrad State University. Together they toured the Hermitage, which houses one of the most stupendous art collections in the world.

The students were well trained in the arts and could converse eloquently as the troupe made their way through the museum. When they came to the famous Rembrandt painting *The Return of the Prodigal Son*, the Soviet students told the story they'd been taught about the painting, which had nothing to do with the biblical account. So Mary, in an effort to clarify what the painting really depicted, told the New Testament story of the prodigal son. The students were fascinated.

Throughout the rest of the tour, they found biblical scene after biblical scene in the famous works of art displayed at the museum, and Mary explained the Bible stories they represented. By the time Mary left Leningrad that first time, the four students had placed their faith in Christ.

Mary phoned me when she got home and exclaimed, "Luci! I taught Sunday school in the Hermitage, and I loved it!"

One of the Russian girls told Mary what it was like to live in the atheistic Soviet Union. "You know, Mary," she said, "what we needed was something for our souls."

If you question the value of the arts, just check with Mary's Russian friends!

The artist is one who looks at life. She's interested and interesting. When a person is interested, she asks herself questions about life. She's curious about her own philosophy. She studies what is in front of her and sees deeper than the outside shell. She wonders. Ponders. Hunts. Turns things over to see what makes them work and of what value they are in the overall scheme of things. And when a person is interesting, she talks about what she has learned in an enjoyable way. What adventures help you capture illumination for your journey?

It's important to hold things loosely—relationships, money, possessions, etc.—because God can always take them away.

_____

_____

_____

_____

_____

_____

_____

_____

_____

_____

_____

_____

_____

_____

_____

_____

_____

_____

_____

Forcing yourself to use restricted means is the sort of restraint that liberates invention. It obliges you to make a kind of progress that you can't even imagine in advance.

—Pablo Picasso

_____

_____

_____

_____

_____

_____

_____

_____

_____

_____

_____

_____

_____

_____

_____

_____

_____

_____

_____

Enlightened moments provide our greatest happiness or greatest wisdom. What are your greatest moments of enlightenment? What do they provide for your life?

A sculptor who worked in a gigantic warehouse roller-skated between peaks of concentration just to relax. With loud music playing, he skated all over the warehouse doing different things—cooking lunch, cleaning up, casting something, grabbing a beer from the fridge, welding, even playing a few tunes on his saxophone while weaving around his studio between work stations. He wrote about that in his journal, and as I read about him, I could see it all in my mind's eye. He said he was "dancing, working, and having a good old time."

The gospel writer with whom I most identify is Luke. He kept a journal. It's called "Acts." And isn't that what we do every day somewhere, alone or with somebody else—act? Well, this old saint was astute enough to capture all those acts in writing. While Matthew, Mark, and John give us amazing insight into the life of Christ, Luke gives us detail. I love detail! I love knowing who went where, who came along, who sat by whom, what they ate, and where they went immediately following dinner. Luke gives us all that info. I just know he kept a journal.

I come from a long line of journal keepers. My mother, grandmother, aunts, and cousins kept little books in which they recorded time and events. Many are filled with pictures and drawings. In some there are challenges or exercises or accounts of their hopes and dreams. I scan these treasured volumes from time to time and get insight into my past—my heritage. I feel myself smiling right now just thinking about those little volumes tucked away in a cedar chest.

Besides God himself, I have no more devoted friend or companion in my life than my journal. I take her everywhere I go, spend time with her, pour out my heart to her, share my burdens and cares, let her see me at my best and worst. I entrust my soul to her keeping. She guards my secrets and lovingly holds my heart. She knows all the dreams I ever dared to entertain.

When I go back to her years later, she's not forgotten a single word. She never filters through my musings, correcting grammar or spelling or editing my honest outpourings. She lets me rant and rave, praise and sing, cry and laugh, giving as much or as little detail as I want, from my own perspective without interrupting. She reflects where I've come from, where I am, and where I want to go. As I look back, I can see how I've changed and grown.

Emerson observed, "The unrecorded life is not worth examining." Why, then, do most of us shy away from recording our lives? Is it too hard? Too time consuming? Too boring? Perhaps that's how you feel. But the private contemplation that journaling provides gives us a place to examine what life really means to us. Within the covers of our own diaries we can be mindful, playful, tearful, or awful. The paper doesn't care. It receives the mood we're in and preserves it for us to look at and learn from. Nothing can take the place of that, and nobody can take it away from us. Every time we chronicle our thoughts and activities, we are verifying our existence and silently thanking God we're alive.

"People travel," Augustine wrote, "to wonder at the height of the mountains, at the huge waves of the seas, at the long course of the rivers, at the vast compass of the ocean, at the circular motion of the stars, and yet they pass by themselves without wondering." It's never too late to start wondering—and writing it all down.

Even though I didn't begin journaling in earnest until 1986, this hobby has become one of my greatest joys. Writing in a journal gives me a place to

report, interpret, argue, reflect, save, question, predict, unload, praise, compare, cry, laugh, draw, paint, and remember. Where else can I do that except at the throne of grace? Nowhere. Getting words on paper lessens pain and fear of the unknown. It's like prayer in many ways. In fact, all my journals contain written prayers. Praying (and journaling) gives me a way to find my own voice and hear God's in response. I don't have to waste a lot of energy on proper sentence structure or editing. I just show up, reflect or unload, and feel better afterward. Sometimes I draw. Bad, funny-looking drawings. Silly drawings. Studied drawings that help me remember how I felt when I broke my leg or had a physical exam or got a tooth filled. Drawings that recall that mountain in the distance, autumn leaves, or a certain bird outside my window.

My journals ask a lot of hypothetical questions where I toy around with answers. On January 1, 1989, I wrote:

If I got on a train and did not know its destination, could I be happy with the trip? Could I just enjoy the going and the interaction with people, not really concerned about the purpose for which I was traveling?

My answer—Yes and No. Something in me needs to know WHY I'm on that train—call it a "higher reason" if you want to, but I'm happier (dare I say happiest) knowing why and where about things. That being the case, my answer is No. But a large part of me simply enjoys the ride—the scenery, the relaxation, the companions on the train. I don't really have to know where I'm going. Both are nice. What does that say about me? I can't make a decision? I don't have to choose? Since I want both, I'm balanced?

This year I want both. To get the most out of the ride, I need to know where and why I'm going as well as have fun along the way.

There are days when I'm so busy living life I don't take time to feel anything. I just go along without thought, trying to get things done. I hate days like that—plodding through duties without being conscious. No sense of purpose. Frankly, I fight that feeling because it's important for me to live fully every moment whenever possible. Hesse said that time "passes like a flash of lightning whose blaze barely lasts long enough to see."[10] I don't want to miss the blaze, so I try very hard to live in the present.

Here are a few journal comments along that line:

June 13, 1989

Someday, when I'm old and gray and a piece of history, will I pull my journals off the shelf and read and reflect and feel the nostalgia that the bittersweet past brings? I wonder. I wonder.

April 18, 1991

Everything changes. That is so true. So enjoy friends, life, love, adventure as it's handed to you. As Pindar once said, "We are things of a day . . . and when the brightness shines on us, life is sweet." So, enjoy the brightness, Luci. All of life has a termination. But while there's brightness with those you love, enjoy it. Remember that it too will pass one day!

March 16, 1995

Sometimes, the passage of time is really hard to grasp. I'm 62 now. Where has it gone . . . all those years? I can't seem to keep up anymore. I can think clearly about time on a daily basis, but lumped together in years, it seems to vanish along the way.

June 25, 1997

Boy! I need to claim a few Scriptures today. I'm feeling my age . . . and older! And, there's always so much to do.

September 8, 2000

My Birthday! I'm 68 today . . . and grateful to God for my rich life. I have salvation and health and friends and love and a beautiful home and a great job and no debts and all I could want. No complaints!

There were a couple times in 2000 that I wrote about being cranky. I just felt out of sorts with the world. If I can get those feelings on paper, it helps me deal with them. As I've said before, seeing something in print or in a drawing enables me to get a better handle on the enemy God and I are fighting.

April 11, 2000

Today I decided I am really cranky. Without meaning to or wanting to, I'm becoming a cranky, irritable old woman. I hate that and am committed to working on it. It's driving me crazy and is maddening to everybody else. Lord, help me!

And again on July 31, 2000

I'm bothered about myself. Why am I so cranky so often?? I pondered that all day. Sometimes I feel trapped in a "calling" but not called. I want to do my thing but am constantly nudged that God wants me to do his thing. I feel resentful toward God for that. I can't stop thinking about it. I asked Mary, Marilyn, and Deb to pray with me about it. I don't like the feeling.

I've also had bouts with depression. Fortunately, they haven't lasted long, but I well recall being very down for no apparent reason. This entry is from June 25, 1991:

Sometimes, in spite of being happy, there is an impending sadness that floods my soul. I've felt it for so many years. I've tried to put a label on it or get a verbal handle on it. I've felt it so deeply at times I could cry. What is it? I don't know. The unbearable lightness of being? Feeling a desire to leap out of my skin . . . all the while bound to earth. An inescapable realization of self. I feel ME. And I felt it today. It seems so out of myself yet so deep within. It's that thing I've often called "cosmic loneliness." It is my flesh—but not my corporeal flesh—it's my nature. It's my _____ . . . ? How can I feel something so deeply and not know what it is? It's the human dilemma.

When I'm in the throes of writing for publication, there are many times I record progress, or regression, in my journal. I write down thoughts to translate into a devotional or book one day, or I simply jot a reminder to myself about the struggle one has as a writer.

Here's a note from October 20, 1997, while I was working on devotionals for the Women of Faith book *We Brake for Joy*:

I've learned something about writing in all this (I think I knew it before but once again was reminded)—even if I don't know what to say keep writing; stay at it; blab on. Then from all that, a kernel of thought emerges; a theme develops, a story line comes to mind, a Scripture is found, and the work is done. The writing is the catharsis that gives birth to the whole thing. What I'm prone to do is feel I have nothing to say so I procrastinate. Remember, Luci—keep at the initial thing: WRITE.

A journal I designed and wrote myself is called *Quite Honestly: A Journal of Thoughts and Activities for Daily Living*. It was a joy to write with my friend Carla Meberg. It's adaptable to any year, divided into months with a theme for each month. On the left side is a place to record one's activities, and on the right, one's thoughts. At the end of each month, there is a place to "Recap."

This journal has been out of print for a long time, but I have one I used in 1990, and I refer to it often. There are quotations, prayers, newspaper clippings, my impressions of art museums, and my thoughts running rampant. I had so much room to think aloud, I wrote like crazy in that book. Here, for example, is a list I made that year of ten things that are important to me. I love rereading it, because even after all this time, everything in it still holds true even though I wrote it years before. This list is a good touchstone for me when my value system gets out of whack.

- It's important that I maintain a strong relationship with God—a direct line of contact and fellowship.
- It's important that the people I love know that, by my generosity and kindness to them. I need to tell them and show them on a consistent basis.
- It's important that I feel safe. I want to take risks and exercise my faith, but to the degree that I'm able, I should keep myself healthy. In this, I should really use my head and best judgment.
- It's important that I am always learning, growing, enlarging my boundaries. It's important that I'm always thinking and asking questions.
- It's important that I work on the areas of my temperament or behavior that I don't like—being jealous or selfish or unforgiving.
- It's important always to be engaged in a project: building something with my hands, writing a book or speech, cleaning up something . . . something where I can lose myself to a cause.
- It's important that I open my heart more and more to the arts—music of all types, art and museums, dance, theater. I want to put my money where my mouth is.
- It's important to have fun—to laugh and sing and joke around. It's important that this kind of spirit permeates my life and my attitude.
- It's important that my time alone be quality, whether I'm resting or not. I don't want to be average in any way. It's always important that my soul be fed.
- It's important to hold things loosely—relationships, money, possessions, etc., because God can always take them away.

Since all of life is a journey, why not write about it along the way? When I considered Emerson's observation—"The unrecorded life is not worth examining"—I took that injunction to heart. I want my life to be both recorded and examined. I want to know what makes me tick.

All my journals are in my library. Not long ago I took a picture of them with a digital camera and made it into a screen saver for my computer. My whole life is in those books. When that picture flashes on the screen, it represents years and years of the adventure of living. I'm glad the Holy Spirit nudged me a long time ago to start writing things down.

My favorite poet is an Englishman named Rupert Brooke. I've read so much of his work—poetry and letters—I feel I know him. Someday I'm sure to find one of his journals tucked away on a dusty shelf in an old bookstore. I keep looking.

Brooke was an adventurer—a graduate of Cambridge, world traveler, officer in the Royal Navy, and one who had an extraordinary gift of self-expression. He wrote about beauty and love and friendship and taking time to live fully. On a spring day in 1912, while traveling in Berlin, he wrote a poem called "The Old Vicarage, Grantchester." The last six lines are the ones I remember most:

> Say, is there Beauty yet to find?
> And Certainty? And Quiet kind
> Deep meadows yet, for to forget
> The lies, and truths, and pain? . . . oh! yet
> Stands the Church clock at ten to three
> And is there honey still for tea?[11]

I painted those lines on a little porcelain tea ball, and each time I have a cup of tea, I read them again, reminding myself to "take time" for beauty, quiet, and certainty. In the trenches of his busy, sometimes dangerous, always adventuresome life, Rupert Brooke took the opportunity to reflect on, examine, and record his thoughts. When he died in 1915 at only twenty-eight years of age, he left us a legacy of words that has been a source of encouragement and joy to me for many years.

I know few people who take adequate time for reflection—and many who regret that they don't. Who said, "The important always gets sacrificed on the altar of the urgent"? Taking time is a better way to live. Rather than racing from one activity to another, let's take our time. Let's reflect on who we are, where we're going, and the life God has given us. Let's live "acts" worth recording—and record them. Who knows what we'll learn and who will learn from our enlightenment in years to come?

Live fully every moment. If we don't live in this moment, we'll lose it and it'll never come again.

If I can get my feelings on paper, it helps me deal with them.

The only way to find your true self is by recklessness and freedom.

—Brenda Ueland

_____

_____

_____

_____

_____

_____

_____

_____

_____

_____

_____

_____

_____

_____

_____

_____

It doesn't take a lot to make me happy—just the right thing.
What makes you happy?

_____

_____

_____

_____

_____

_____

_____

_____

_____

_____

_____

_____

_____

_____

_____

_____

_____

_____

How does one remember what happens as the years come and go?
When does one know what is important rather than trivial?
What can one do to keep the memories from fading?

One of the best gifts Mother gave me was an appreciation for the fun of hospitality and the joy of friendship. She modeled both in every way. She was a people person, plain and simple. She loved big gatherings, and could Mother throw a party!

In my junior year of high school I was invited to sing with a little band made up of Mr. Seastrand's students at the year-end dance. Mother said, "Just be home by 11:30. We'll be up 'cause we're having a party here . . . a barbecue in the backyard."

"You are? Who's coming? Why didn't I know this?"

"Well, your dad and I just thought of it a couple of days ago. We've asked a few neighbors, friends from church. We've also lined up a clown who'll come and do a few antics . . . then that guy down the street—the one that 'eats fire'—is coming when the clown finishes. It's some trick he learned during the war. But you have fun, honey, and we'll see ya later."

Hey. Wait just a minute here! Do I really want to leave?

I was picked up by one of the guys in the band, and off we went. I hung out with my friends for a while, then sang my numbers with the group, but all I could think about was a clown and a fire-eater in my backyard. I asked my friend to take me home.

It was about ten o'clock, and the yard was teeming with people. They were laughing and singing, eating hot dogs and barbecue, having a great ol' time. Mother and Daddy greeted me sweetly and asked if I had enjoyed myself. They never questioned my getting home early or what was up. It was as though I was supposed to be there all along, and they simply included me with no questions asked. I got home in time to see the clown, the fire-eater, and all my pals from church.

As far back as I can remember, Mother had friends and was constantly inviting them to dinner or parties at our house, to meet at church, come over for coffee, play forty-two, go shopping, or (on occasion) come with us on family vacations. Whatever ... she was Momo reincarnated, gathering up folks who wanted or needed companionship, and she genuinely enjoyed their company. Mother was the personification of *joie de vivre*. Her heart and her life were rich with meaningful friendships. In that respect, I wanted to be like her.

I wanted to try my hand at "eating fire", too. Trust me! It's hard to do —

Friendship is a wonderful thing. I cannot imagine a day going by without talking with my friends. In fact, as I sit here working, trying to put words together in a meaningful way, it would be a lot easier if I were writing an e-mail to Debbie or Jan or Mary or Pat. The words would flow without hesitation or forethought. I'd rather be talking on the phone with Ney or Marilyn ... or jotting a letter to Kurt or Julius or Cyndi. I could just say whatever came to mind. Any way I'd want to put it would be fine with any one of my true friends.

Victoria, TX.

FROM DEEP IN THE HEART OF TEXAS

Speaker   Celeb

How do   you spell relief? O-V-E-R
Ye! I'm all   through speaking here-
An engagement that's been on my
calendar so many years — and now it's over!
Just as tone if I'm glad. Oh my. But... they were
a lovely, responsive, Texas audience. In fact, there
was a whole row of women from El Campo. I asked
them to stand. One woman brought me a copy of
my mother's High School graduating seniors, & her name
is 73 years old. The woman who gave it to me baby sat
was a friend of Isabell Sokolosky (I remember mothe
it was among Isabell's things that this list was b
here for safe keeping! I've said a hundred tim
warm, responsive, pretty & appreciative. Ab

I also want to tell you about ordering breakfas
told me it was okay — that Denny's knew. I called abou
Room 108." Dead silence — Finally, "Ma'am... this is
La Quinta." I finally talked to "Connie" who said she k
This Class Roll is 73 yrs. old →

me breakfa

A g
gra
of u

I de
clo
At
Go
res
clo
me
the
Kid
— ju
the

Sat

me
&

mother's High School graduating class roll from 1925. Her
Lovell Lucille Lundy. Isabel Reeves was her best friend.

CLASS MOTTO

"Be Sure You are Right, Then go Ahead."

CLASS FLOWER   CLASS COLORS
Moss and Rose   Old Rose and Grey

CLASS ROLL

Willie Anthis   Jewell Agnes Hensley
Bernice Bard   Irene Parr Johnson
Verna Boyd   Annie Rosalie Kainer
Lee Ray Brod   Theodore Kubesch
Lillie Mae Cervenka   Lovell Lucille Lundy
Oscar Arvie Charnquist   Velma Mae MacWilliams
Florence Comstock   George Pleasant Willis
James Elmer Cornett   Ernestine Spoerl
Wendell Percy Cummings   Henley Webb
Edwin Dahl   Isabel Reeves
George Dixon   Hattie Belle Orrick
Viola Ehman   Chloe Mozelle Roades
Mary Esther Ellison   J. Earle Shackelford
Vasil S. Heiler   Clyde M. Shaver

In a beautiful essay on friendship, Ralph Waldo Emerson asserted that there are two cornerstones foundational to friendship. One is truth, the other tenderness. I agree. To love someone, we must know he or she is truthful with us. Love is built on respect and respect on truth. Truth and tenderness must go hand in hand, because if they try to stand alone, one will be too hard and the other too soft.

I would add a third element that is essential to friendship—freedom. We can love others tenderly, be completely truthful with them, but unwittingly want them as our own. We find ourselves hurt if they do things with other people and we're not included. If we don't encourage them to be free (even of us), there is no real friendship. "The condition which high friendship demands is the ability to do without it," Emerson says. When we hold on to anything too tightly, it dies. We kill it in the grip of our will.

Learning to let people be free has been hard for me—especially when I was younger and insecure about myself. I was afraid that if I allowed my friends to fly, pursue their own dreams, differ with me in basic tenets, then we couldn't remain friends. I feared they would find somebody they loved more, and I'd be left in the lurch. But I was completely wrong. Actually, the opposite is true. I've learned that when we open our hands, our arms, our hearts, and let freedom ring, those we love will want to be with us—because we don't demand it of them. Milan Kundera sums up what I'm trying to say so well:

> Perhaps all the questions we ask of love, to measure, test, probe, and save it, have the additional effect of cutting it short. Perhaps the reason we are unable to love is that we yearn to be loved, that is, we demand something . . . instead of delivering ourselves up to him demand-free and asking for nothing but his company.[12]

Frankly, I think relationships are even hard to write about. And not only are they hard to put into words, but they're hard to maintain. One of the greatest tests of character is to be loving and gracious when we'd rather not. When Scripture tells us "a friend loves at all times," we may want that, but the ability to do it has to come from the Lord. The human heart is selfish, prefers its own way, fights being molded by God, and doesn't want to give in when we don't get what is "rightfully ours." We're stubborn, prideful, and strong-willed, and these unbecoming characteristics are most starkly revealed in our relationships.

When I think of my closest friendships—those in which I've grown, learned to compromise and negotiate, established boundaries—I notice that in every case they were built on a mutual ability to let each other be free. Free to investigate, explore, or embrace something that did not necessarily appeal to both persons. And I've learned this lesson from my friends—by their tender truthfulness with me.

I recall times of jealousy toward those closest to me, hating it in myself but seemingly unable to rise above it. I would pout, walk out, ignore, speak out of turn—in short, act like a petulant child. But because my friends cared enough about me and our friendship, they lovingly pointed out the problem with my behavior and the lack of grounds for my feelings. I had to work it through, though. They couldn't do it for me.

I still work at it and will as long as I'm in the human condition, I'm sure. People may not be aware of all my internal struggles, because I've learned, through much practice, to resist dumping the whole truck on some unsuspecting victim. But I believe I'll always have times that I behave badly because I don't get my way, and I'll have to fight against acting like the jerk I really am. I'll have to count to ten and unload my gun at the foot of the cross. Otherwise, who'll be able to stand being around me?

For me, one of the hardest things is being told what to do. I hate that. What somebody thinks I need. How I should change. That I should get over it, grow up, stand down, back off, or just shut up. Truth hurts. But there's a way to dispense it that is acceptable—and biblical.

"As iron sharpens iron, so one man sharpens another," says Proverbs 27:17. What a great verse. It came to mind not long ago when I was sharpening a knife in the kitchen. I'd been trying to slice a tomato and had almost hacked the thing to mush. Finally, it hit my numb skull that the knife needed a good sharpening. Duh. I took out a whetstone and had at it. In no time it was a razor, slicing that tomato beautifully. Metal met metal, and that which was dull and ineffective was once again functioning at high efficiency.

That's friendship whetted by truth. Without a willingness to recognize our own shortcomings, value correction, or set about changing and growing up, friendship will simply die. Of dullness! It will have no value.

One thing that's consistently invigorating and helps us know another person is to address philosophical quandaries together. Here is a list of some of the questions my friends and I have considered together through the years:

- *What are the five things you want most out of life?*
- *What possible situation could wrench you out of being your true self?*
- *What are the absolutes of your life—things that won't ever change?*
- *What's the difference between hypocritical and political, and where does integrity lie in both? (I love this question—it's from my friend Marilyn!)*
- *If you could change one thing in your life, what would it be?*
- *Do you believe logic is subjective or objective? Why?*
- *What is a "wonderful life"? Do you have one?*
- *How does a person turn theory into practicality?*
- *Name your three greatest areas of need. To what degree can I meet those?*

There are many more questions where these come from. Our discussions have given us opportunity to know each other better without spotlighting problem areas, per se. The whole idea is to use the questions as a springboard to get to the heart of our own issues and problems and to bring light into dark areas that need attention. Philosophical musings give us a place to start addressing trouble spots in our friendships and in ourselves.

I can tell you from experience that I honestly don't know where I would be today if my friends hadn't loved me enough to point out inappropriate things in me that needed attention. If we're not willing to rely on the love, honesty, and caring of our friends and loved ones to "sharpen" us, we'll wind up a menace to the rest of the human race. And we'll drive ourselves into a corner of loneliness, because no one will want to be with us unless they're planning to kill us. Trust me on this! I've met lots of folks unwilling to change maddening behavior, and they are an unadulterated pain. A trial to be around, and who wants to? Life's too short to spend time with them.

I found this old quote by Sir Walter Raleigh in an 1853 edition of *Great Truths by Great Authors*:

Thou mayst be sure that he that will in private tell thee of thy faults, is thy Friend, for he adventures thy dislike, and doth hazard thy hatred; for there are few men that can endure it, every man for the most part delighting in self-praise, which is one of the most universal follies that bewitcheth Mankind.

Don't you love "adventures thy dislike" and "bewitcheth Mankind"? For this kind of friendship, I thank God, and I thank that handful of loving folks who know what to say to me and how and when to say it, and for the fact that they do it kindly and in the spirit of grace. If you've got friends like that, praise God for them every day of your life. You're rich.

One brief caution before I move on: If friends are unable or unwilling to change when truth is presented to them about troublesome characteristics, just know this—you can't change them. It's not possible. You can present the problem, pray about it, hope for the best, but the change occurs only when a person wants to be different. Otherwise, forget it and leave it alone. Only time, experience, and God can change any of us for the better.

Mother told me once when I wanted to give up on a friendship that wasn't going my way to look at it from the other person's point of view. She said something like, "You can't make people into what you want them to be. People are themselves. They're cut out of their own cloth. Try to think about what you can give them, not what they can give you." That was good advice. And she was an example of that to her friends.

We had neighbors all around us who didn't know the Lord, and Mother

Momo and me

never stopped doing good, listening to their troubles, or giving love to them in Jesus' name. When Thelma Roberts, a neighbor and close friend, was widowed and had no children to step in, Mother cared for her the remainder of her life. Mother invited Thelma to Bible class; she declined, and Mother didn't insist. After a while, though, she asked if the invitation still stood, and in no time, Mother personally introduced Thelma to Jesus Christ.

Thelma told me shortly before she passed away that my mother had saved her life. "She reached out to me when I had nobody else. She just never stopped giving, and she never asked anything of me. I owe her my life. What a friend!"

Thelma captured exactly what Jesus said in John 15:13, "Greater love has no one than this, that he lay down his life for his friends." Mother laid down her life for her friend, and in the end, the friend found eternal life because of what Mother modeled.

True friendships are characterized by grace, truth, forgiveness, unselfishness, boundaries, care, and love in gigantic and mutual proportion. Although they require hard work and consistency from each party, we enjoy the best of the best in life because when friends come alongside, more light is added to our paths. Two are better than one! We lay down our lives for our friends, they lay down their lives for us, and in the end we all find true life.

I love the way God thinks. I learned it from my mother.

Nothing is wasted. The good, the bad, the ugly, and the things we think will kill us. God uses it all, and he develops our purpose out of the stuff in our trash. He sifts through it, shows us how to tell it, and then helps others with it. We all meet in our own humanity. How has God enriched you to help others?

_____

_____

_____

_____

_____

_____

_____

_____

_____

_____

_____

_____

_____

_____

_____

_____

_____

_____

_____

_____

_____

_____

_____

_____

_____

_____

_____

_____

_____

_____

_____

_____

_____

_____

_____

_____

_____

_____

_____

_____

_____

When we ask ourselves hypothetical questions, we, in effect,
reestablish who we are and validate the fact that it's okay to be ourselves.

Learning to be content is an educational process just like all learning. It takes time.

When my heart condemns me and cries, "You have done it again," I am to believe God again as to the value of the finished work of Jesus Christ.

—Francis Schaeffer

_____

_____

_____

_____

_____

_____

_____

_____

_____

_____

_____

_____

_____

_____

_____

_____

_____

_____

_____

_____

_____

_____

PART 4

CAPTURING THE ESSENCE

CANON EOS
w/35-70mm 1:3.5-4.5

PART 4

CAPTURING THE ESSENCE

"This is the victory that has overcome the world, even our faith. Who is it that overcomes the world? Only he who believes that Jesus is the Son of God" (1 John 5:4–5). I love those two verses. They are the hallmark of the child of God and for years were my favorite verses in the Bible. In a nutshell they sum up one's relationship with Christ—the Victor!

During the Hellenistic period of Greek history, a piece of sculpture was produced that is the essence of a Christian's life of faith. The sculptor didn't plan that at the time, of course, but seeing it always reminds me that as a Christian, I am an overcomer. The piece of sculpture is called the *Nike of Samothrace*, more widely known as *The Winged Victory*. And here's a dab of history that will set it in place. The Hellenistic Age in the Mediterranean area and Near East lasted approximately 290 years. It began with the premature death of Alexander the Great and lasted until Rome sacked Egypt. During this period, Greek art hit its zenith. It changed dramatically from the earlier Classical Era. There was more pronounced realism and expressiveness. Statues struck a pose instead of being static and uninteresting. Drapery covered heretofore-stylized figures, as though it was blowing in the breeze. All sculpture took on new drama and movement.

Nike of Samothrace was sculpted from marble around 190 BC. Excavations have shown that initially it was placed alighting on a flagship, set in the ground on a high hill in such a way that it appeared to float. It was as if this enormous figure had just descended to the prow of the ship for all sailors and pilgrims to see from a distance as they approached the port of Samothrace. *Nike* means "victory," and to catch sight of a great goddess with wings spread wide against her foes was no doubt a source of encouragement for all.

"THE DOCTRINE OF DIVINE ESSENCE"

"God is able to touch the Political, Civil, &
Military Leaders of the Nations of the
Earth, tho' they be far from Him."
Dr. S. Lewis Johnson
7-31-57

T II 56   187X

When the statue was discovered in modern times (1863), it still radiated strength and majesty, in spite of the fact it had lost its head and both arms somewhere along the way. Today it stands in the Louvre in Paris, at the top of an ascending staircase, exuding magnificence, power, and victory. Even in its damaged state it expresses triumph. When Cézanne saw it for the first time in Paris, he wrote a friend, "I do not need to see the head to imagine her gaze, because all the blood that courses and flows through her legs, hips, and every part of her body, has rushed through her brain to her heart. When the head broke off, the marble surely bled."

I bought a huge poster of the *Nike of Samothrace* several years ago when I was in the Louvre and had it framed. It hangs in my living room and daily serves as a reminder that through Christ I am victorious. I am Nike, because through Christ's strength I can overcome the ill winds and foes that would attack me.

Actually, I like the fact that the sculpture has no head and arms. Never having seen what they looked like anyway, the figure seems complete. This massive, strong, female body of marble is steadfast and elegant, without a trace of fear of defeat. There's no head to change its mind, no arms to rise in surrender. The *Winged Victory* captures the essence of my life with Christ.

the ledger, even by ...
n" (all Homo Sapiens) are born ...
an is born dead, in sin he canno...
Holy God, who cannot look upon ...
alty of sin is death, & the pe...
Christ "bought us" by paying ...
he Cross, & the moment we put ...
"made alive," Spiritually. Before ...
iteousness which is as filthy rags" ...
Rom. 3:23), or, as we say "—R" ...

One of the benefits of growing up in a Christian home was an early expo-sure to God's Word. I can hardly remember a day when somebody in the family wasn't reading the Bible or talking about it. It was as commonplace as eating, going to school, or doing chores, and I'll go to my grave being grateful for that.

The Bible is an amazing volume of work—like no other! In sixty-six books there is perfect historical continuity from the creation of the world to the new heaven and new earth. Truths constantly unfold, prophecy is ful-filled, and the most perfect Person on earth or in heaven is anticipated, presented, realized, and exalted. This collection of authors—kings, peasants, philosophers, physicians, fishermen, statesmen, poets, and plowmen—couldn't have known much about each other because they lived in various countries and their writings extended over sixty generations of human his-tory, representing sixteen hundred years—yet the Bible all fits together. The book is a phenomenon without question, and it is utterly inexhaustible. It sweeps across the heights of heaven to the depths of hell, tracing the works of God from beginning to end. Voltaire, the French infidel who died in 1778, predicted the Bible would be obsolete within a hundred years, but here we are in the twenty-first century proving him wrong. The Bible endures. And not only does it endure; its truth continues to transform lives.

Although all that is true, it wasn't until I was a young adult that I real-ized this book offered a great deal more than just the plan for salvation. It incorporated everything I needed to live a meaningful, rich life. When I started going to Bible classes with my parents four nights a week, a whole new world opened, and for the first time I began to understand numerous benefits that were mine simply because I had put my faith in Jesus Christ. I could actually learn and apply these facts in my daily life in a way that really made a difference. I didn't have to be knocked down by every wind that blew across my emotional path, because I had a fortress and buffer in God's Word as sturdy as the Winged Victory. That buffer was called doctrine.

Essentially, doctrine is the raw material of Scripture that informs and counsels us in formulating theological truth. As I began to study, I learned it wasn't something only seminary students understood, but I could get it too. It is available to every Christian. First Timothy 4:16 says, "Watch your life and doctrine closely. Persevere in them, because if you do, you will save both yourself and your hearers." When I found that verse, I discovered the first of many pearls that were to become mine as I kept digging for treasure.

There are ten basic doctrines every child of God should have some knowledge of and on which we can stake our lives. (Somebody should write *Doctrines Every Child Should Know.*) If we understand these, even in a rudimentary way, we won't be forced to live according to our emotions alone. Our feelings will enter in, of course, and find their place, but we'll be able to stand on an immovable, unchanging foundation we can trust.

Hundreds of books have been written about these topics:

Bibliology—Doctrine of the Bible
Theology—Doctrine of God the Father
Christology—Doctrine of God the Son
Pneumatology—Doctrine of God the Spirit
Angelology—Doctrine of Angels
Anthropology—Doctrine of Man
Hamartiology—Doctrine of Sin
Soteriology—Doctrine of Salvation
Ecclesiology—Doctrine of the Church
Eschatology—Doctrine of the End Times

This is a nice, tidy list that helps me know there is a sequence to learning God's Word, starting with the doctrine of the Bible and going to the doctrine of the end times. I learn best when I follow simple outlines. In 1 Corinthians 14:40 the apostle Paul says, "Everything should be done in a fitting and orderly way," and I think that's what this list does. It puts biblical truth in an understandable sequence. It's the raw material that gives me solid ground from which to view the events that shape my life as a Christian.

But how does the unfolding of these seemingly antiquated precepts help me to live in today's world? How can knowing this stuff keep me from being dismayed about circumstances, point me in the right direction when the chips are down, or encourage me to depend on what God says rather than on how I feel?

Well, look, for example, at theology. It has to do, in great part, with God's attributes—what I like to call his "essence." These are the divine characteristics that form his makeup. God is eternal, infinite, sovereign, omnipotent, omniscient, omnipresent, and immutable. In addition, he is perfect love, grace, patience, and compassion. He's holy, righteous, just, and faithful. God is all of these things every day, all the time, and I can count on it because it says so in the Bible, and I believe the Bible to be absolutely true. (If you want to get down to the nitty-gritty of whether we can believe the Bible, study the doctrine of Bibliology.)

By the same token, if God the Father has all these attributes, so does God the Son and God the Holy Spirit, because they are three in one. All that applies to one applies to the others as well. (Again, the doctrine of theology.)

Hebrews 13:8 proclaims, "Jesus Christ is the same yesterday and today and forever." Psalm 33:11 affirms, "But the plans of the LORD stand firm forever, the purposes of his heart through all generations." And Malachi 3:6 states simply but emphatically, "I the LORD do not change." All three of these Scriptures are doctrinal statements. They are true no matter how I feel, on a good day or a bad day, if I get what I want or don't. They're firm, trustworthy, and constant. Forever.

One example of how knowing these doctrinal truths has helped me continues to play itself out every day in just one aspect of my life—living alone. I've lived by myself for the past forty years, and it's been an interesting adventure. More often than not, there's been nobody in the wings to come to my aid financially, nobody to pick up the slack or run errands when I've dragged my body home tired and defeated, and nobody to lift me out of the doldrums. Humanly speaking, all responsibility ultimately has fallen on me. Some days I feel okay about this; other days I don't—I feel over-whelmed. But the days keep coming no matter how I feel, just as they do for you . . . whether you live by yourself or not. I can choose to let my over-whelming feelings guide my behavior (and sometimes I do), or I can choose to believe that God is with me and caring for me and teaching me lessons I couldn't learn any other way. *Settle down and accept things as they are, Lucille. Remember . . . this, too, shall pass.*

If I choose to live out of my emotions, no telling what might happen or where I might go to salve my depression, dissatisfaction, or discouragement. Feelings fluctuate with the day, the wind, my hormones, circumstances, and human relationships. But because God told me he doesn't change, I can choose to believe him no matter how I feel. This is what I mean about liv-ing out of doctrine rather than feelings.

But let's say I don't choose to do this. Let's say I've had enough of this academic way of looking at life and decide to take matters into my own hands. I'm tired of waiting for God to answer my prayers, so I do whatever I want. Forget doctrine! I'm outta here.

I'm sick of living alone as a single woman, so my lover and I move in together.

I want to drive a nicer car because I think it will help my image, so I run up a hefty debt buying it on credit, even though my outgo is already more than my income.

I give myself a hard look in the mirror one day and don't like what I see, so I begin buying lots of beautiful clothes (again on credit) to feel better about myself.

I get a face-lift and a tummy tuck and start hanging around with "beau-tiful people." Maybe someone will notice me for a change.

I've been dying to set somebody straight because she wronged me, so I meet with her and tell her off. Actually, it feels downright good to get it out of my system.

On and on and on. You can imagine your own scenario. Whatever feels good, do it. This is what we're told every day in a hundred different ways and from a hundred different sources.

I have to admit, every one of these desires has at some time crossed my mind. And that's the whole point. I'm not denigrating the feelings and desires that cross our minds. Feelings aren't what do us in, though they constantly demand satisfaction. We are done in when we live out of these ever-changing feelings. And if we have no doctrinal truths under our belt and know nothing about God's Word, how else can we live? We aren't in a vacuum, folks—we make decisions from somewhere inside.

But that seems like a dry and boring way to live, you may say, inconsequential in the long run. Life is passing me by, and if I don't do these things, it will be over and I will have missed the boat and had no fun. Don't I know it. I've felt that way too. But life is going to go right on whether we follow our hearts or our heads. That's a given. Unless the Lord returns right away, we have to live our lives every day. So—what are we going to do?

Since I'm looking back on most of my life, I know from experience what I'm going to do. To the degree I'm able, I'm going to strive for both. I'm going to live out of my head and my heart. I want to live out of truth, tenderness, and freedom. While I don't advocate following only your heart because that can take you off course, neither do I advocate being so strict with yourself that you miss the joy of life. Yes, by obeying Scripture you will miss some things—fun things—once-in-a-lifetime things. Nevertheless, there will be more peace and tranquillity in your spirit if you weigh your desires more heavily on the side of God. This Scripture is true: "The mind of sinful man is death, but the mind controlled by the Spirit is life and peace" (Romans 8:6).

Even though there will always be a battle between what we know to do and what we prefer to do, there are ways to have a full, meaningful, adventuresome, rich life and—trust me on this—lots of fun. It lies in overcoming the addiction of doing only what feels good.

Proverbs 14:12–13 says, "There is a way that seems right to a man, but in the end it leads to death. Even in laughter the heart may ache, and joy may end in grief." Sadly, yes. Doing certain things to relieve the agonies of the spirit can feel so right at the time, fulfilling and fun, but when we go that route, there is hell to pay in the end because we have gotten out of sync with God. Our foolish choices will haunt us, as that verse implies.

Therefore, here's what I've done in place of the but-it-feels-so-good scenario:

Instead of taking a lover, I've chosen to believe God's love is more satisfying than any other. Scripture tells me, "Because your love is better than life, my lips will glorify you" (Psalm 63:3). Sound boring? Maybe some days, but it's better for me in the long run.

Instead of running up debt and hanging with the "right people," I try very hard to rely on the fact that God isn't interested in my image; he's concerned with my heart. Scripture tells me, "Man looks at the outward appearance, but the Lord looks at the heart" (1 Samuel 16:7). The choice of where to place my focus is mine.

Instead of taking matters into my own hands and telling off the person who has hurt me, I elect to wait and let God handle it his way. Scripture tells me, "Do not take revenge, my friends, but leave room for God's wrath, for it is written: 'It is mine to avenge; I will repay,' says the Lord" (Romans 12:19). For God's child, this is by far the better way.

Nothing about the choices I'm describing is easy. Not at first anyway. I don't have to tell you that living by your feelings can be exhilarating. But sinful behavior never fully satisfies the heart. There are momentary pleasures, but the end is death—death of a friendship, death of one's health, death of one's finances, death of a romance, death of a dream, and ultimately, death of the body.

I can sum it all up by saying that the truths of the Bible have saved my life. Knowing Scripture has enabled me to overcome many odds. God's truth has spared me much of the heartache that occurs when I operate only out of what feels good or what I'd rather be doing. And, God knows, I'm not speaking from some lofty place—I know this from experience. I've had lots of heartache because I, like every human being, have made foolish choices and suffered the consequences.

My greatest challenge in life along this line has been with those whom I have loved the most. These are the ones from whom I have felt the deepest hurt. Total strangers don't affect me that much. They can say what they want, they can criticize or accuse me, and while that might cause a momentary pang, it really doesn't matter. It's water off a duck's back. It's the same with casual acquaintances—when they hurt my feelings, there's nothing in me that wants to get even or carry a grudge because I don't care that much. For the most part, my basic temperament is laid back. In that, I'm like my dad.

But when someone to whom I have entrusted my heart does something to cause me pain, I react. I might not say anything to that person, but the villainy in me rises up to seek vindication. I look for ways to inflict punishment. Nothing in me wants to forgive them or try to see the other person's side. I might be silently bleeding to death in the corner, but I want that person to know it is he or she who has caused the bleeding.

A number of years ago a dear friend betrayed me by misrepresenting me to mutual friends and acquaintances. I felt her words caused irreparable damage to my reputation. It was horrible. I ached inside like I was going to die. I never confronted this person about what she had done, because confrontation is so hard for me. Outwardly, I ignored what she did and kept silent. But inwardly I held a grudge—sat in the corner and bled to death. I did everything I could to get back at her. I detached, withheld forgiveness and love, and did all the things Jesus wouldn't do. I was hurt, it was her fault, and in my opinion, she deserved my bad spirit toward her. It was as simple as that.

A breach settled in that lasted twenty-five years. During that time I moved several states away, and since we were miles apart emotionally as well as geographically, I wasn't forced to reconcile, so I didn't. But I couldn't forget what had happened. The pain of her actions and the disease of my own self-righteous grudge haunted me. I tried to ignore it. But as the psalmist says,

> *When I kept silent,*
> *my bones wasted away*
> *through my groaning all day long.*
> *For day and night*
> *your hand was heavy upon me;*
> *my strength was sapped*
> *as in the heat of summer. (Psalm 32:3–4)*

As the years passed, I finally realized I was wrong. It no longer mattered that I had been hurt; it mattered that I was living a lie. I was professing God's truth but denying its power. It wouldn't be an exaggeration to say I hated my friend. And I hated what that hate was doing to me. I knew it was a violation of everything I believe.

I decided to face the fact that out of sight is never really out of mind when it comes to something God intends for us to deal with. Obviously, I wasn't meant to just get away from the person who had hurt me. Geographical distance is never an excuse for selfish behavior. Besides, being apart didn't alleviate the pain I felt. I had locked myself in a prison of my own making and thrown away the key. I felt helpless. So I did the only thing I knew to do. I poured my heart out to God. Because Jesus was human, he knew how I felt; and because he was divine, he had the power to forgive those feelings. This was basic doctrinal teaching, doctrine I had studied for years and on which I had based my life. With King David I prayed:

> *Have mercy on me, O God,*
> *according to your unfailing love;*
> *according to your great compassion*
> *blot out my transgressions.*

Wash away all my iniquity
and cleanse me from my sin.
For I know my transgressions,
and my sin is always before me.
Against you, you only, have I sinned
and done what is evil in your sight,
so that you are proved right when you speak
and justified when you judge. (Psalm 51:1–4)

It took a while, but in time something inside me started to change. The shell around my heart began to crack open. I felt more charitable toward my friend. I found I wanted to make things right, whatever "right" meant. I didn't want to sit around anymore waiting for her to see the error of her ways. I slowly, slowly began to heal.

During this time, I had occasion to return to the city where my friend lived, and I phoned her to ask if we could have lunch. She was a bit stunned but agreed. We met and talked and actually enjoyed visiting. She never brought up the breach, and neither did I. The healing God had done in my heart enabled me to relate to her with a love that came from him. I no longer focused on what she'd done to me. I focused on God, who was miraculously infusing me with a forgiving spirit toward her. It was amazing how my change of focus altered everything. As a Roman emperor wrote, "When you are offended at anyone's fault, turn to yourself and study your own failings. By attending to them, you will forget your anger and learn to live wisely."

Over time, God kept nudging me to do something more tangible to demonstrate a spirit of reconciliation. *Go the extra mile, Lucille.* How many times had I learned and lived that mantra? I knew deep inside that it was God's will for me, both in general and in this specific relationship. And so I began. I had an idea and pursued it. Because my friend had always loved traveling but no longer could because of ill health, I decided to send her postcards from every city I visited. For the next four years I did just that— 104 postcards in all. She put those cards everywhere. Her refrigerator was lined with them, and two shoe boxes held the rest. Most of the cards were not from faraway places with strange-sounding names. Where they were from didn't matter. Even if I'd written them all from my own backyard, it would have been okay. What my friend loved was being remembered. And what I loved was remembering her. She told me she lived for that correspondence. They often came on days when her physical prognosis looked bleak, and they cheered her up. She read them to friends on the phone and studied the stamps. She haunted the mailbox just to be sure she didn't miss any.

In December 2000 my friend died. She had kept all the cards, and upon her death they were returned to me by her thoughtful family. I will always keep those cards and treasure that legacy in friendship. I've reread them, remembering the moment each was written. Most of all, I reflected on how valuable it had been to make a genuine effort to be everything I hadn't been but could be for this person from whom I had been estranged for so long. I cannot tell you how grateful I am for those last few years in our relationship. And the interesting irony is that we never once talked about the breach that kept us apart so long. It had simply disappeared into the woodwork of life.

I'm grateful for what my actions did for my friend, but my gratitude goes much deeper than that. I'm mostly grateful for what God did for me. Many years ago, I learned the truth about God doctrinally. He is all grace, and his Spirit dwells in me. What I cannot do for myself, he can do. He can turn the principles of doctrine into everyday reality. He can extend love, grace, and forgiveness to another through me. And he doesn't do it because the person deserves it or because I deserve to have it done. He does it to set me free—free from sin, free from guilt, free from myself! The sin of my friend kept me bound to pious hypocrisy. When I brought all of that to the Savior, he took it away. He replaced my heart of stone with a heart of love. Who won? I did. She did. He did. His kingdom did. We all did. I couldn't have done it on my own or for myself.

Ever since that day of coming face-to-face with my hard and vengeful heart, I've realized my soul is a "terrible and dangerous coil spring," as Nikos Kazantzakis says. I am a very human being. Each of us carries within us falsehood, self-centeredness, cowardice, and the capacity to do unbelievably unkind things to others. As long as we are in the human condition, that will be the case. How grateful I am that our gracious God stooped down in the person of Christ to save us from ourselves and reconcile us to himself! As the apostle Paul wrote:

> *I realize that I don't have what it takes. I can will it, but I can't do it. . . .*
> *I've tried everything and nothing helps. I'm at the end of my rope. Is there no one who can do anything for me? Isn't that the real question?*
> *The answer, thank God, is that Jesus Christ can and does. He acted to set things right in this life of contradictions where I want to serve God with all my heart and mind, but am pulled by the influence of sin to do something totally different. (Romans 7:18, 24–25 MSG)*

Life is hard; no doubt about it. But in it there's lots of depth to be explored and growth to be experienced. That's all part of the adventure. For me personally, exploring, knowing, and experiencing starts and ends with the fact that Jesus loves me. He tells me so. And it is that divine love that transforms the human heart.

I don't always get God's truth exactly right, and sometimes I'm way off, but I do believe a great part of doing life differently is nourished at the well of having built my foundation on solid doctrinal truth. Apart from that there is too much emotional pain in life for me to keep going, too much remorse to pick up the pieces, too difficult a path ahead to keep trucking down the road.

In the fourth chapter of Ephesians (one of my favorite books, by the way), starting at verse 14, Paul writes:

> *We will no longer be infants, tossed back and forth by the waves, and blown here and there by every wind of teaching and by the cunning and craftiness of men in their deceitful scheming. Instead, speaking the*

truth in love, we will in all things grow up into him who is the Head,
that is, Christ.

What a wonderful mouthful of doctrine! Paul says we're strong adults who know how to tenderly speak the truth. Christ is our leader, and because of that we don't ever have to waver in our beliefs. We are secure in him.

In my lifetime, I've seen thousands of fads come and go, philosophies of life change like the weather, political systems overturned in revolutions. Nothing stays steady. Except God! The essence of his being is always the same: yesterday, today, and forever. We can trust him and his Word. If we live to be 110, or if the world explodes tomorrow, we can count on him. When we bank our life on that truth and "grow up into him who is the Head," we will be stable, secure, and immovable in our faith.

The Word of God is powerful enough to change
darkness to light and dissatisfaction to joy.
How has God's Word transformed you or your outlook on life?

_____

_____

_____

_____

_____

_____

_____

_____

_____

_____

_____

_____

_____

_____

_____

_____

_____

Don't manipulate God; just receive. Communion with him isn't something you institute. It's like sleep. You can't make yourself sleep, but you can create the conditions that allow sleep to happen. Create those conditions for receiving God: open your Bible, read it slowly, listen to it, and reflect on it.

—Richard Foster

What is it about the Bible that catches us off guard . . . that reaches into the depths of our souls and little by little begins straightening us out?

_____

_____

_____

_____

_____

_____

_____

_____

_____

_____

_____

_____

_____

_____

_____

_____

_____

_____

Not forgiving is like drinking rat poison
and then waiting for the rat to die.

—*Anne Lamott*

_____

_____

_____

_____

_____

_____

_____

_____

_____

_____

_____

_____

_____

_____

_____

_____

_____

_____

Foundational doctrinal truths laid down in "yesterday" provide rich soil in which to plant seeds needed for today's emotional and spiritual growth. Head knowledge alone does not encompass the essence of what life is all about. Rather, it is a necessary ingredient for what God wants to manifest in our hearts. Knowing truth alone can never make my heart soft. It will never produce warmth or a caring spirit. And the old saying has great merit: "People don't care how much you know unless they know how much you care."

As a matter of fact, too much data makes me weary. Even if it's all true. Spare me the loquacious person who goes on and on about anything. As much as I love words, I find people like that tedious. Give me somebody with soul. Show me the person who can melt my heart, who is tender and sweet—but not given to maudlin sentimentality and hollow drama. I'll follow him or her to the ends of the earth.

So, where's the balance between head and heart? How do we establish ourselves firmly in the unshakable foundation of truth and at the same time feel things deeply? The integration of what we think with how we feel affords a rich, authentic spiritual life and ensures meaningful connections with others. But where do we find the formula? Is there one?

As simplistic as it sounds, we find it in relationship to God. He created us—will, intellect, and emotions. Scripture says we are complete in him. By nature, I'm more cerebral than emotional. I have friends who are just the opposite. And I've known folks with wills like steel, but they don't necessarily think straight or care. Individuals who are out of sync with the way they were created can be maddening. But none of us can create within ourselves that harmonious blend that echoes the essential ground of our being in Christ. Only our Maker can synthesize us and make us whole. When we find our center, when our identity is in him, when the core of our being revolves around him, we're not just academic (as I tend to be) or emotional (like

Winnie-the-Pooh's friend Eeyore) or willful (like a two-year-old I once knew). We're whole because he's made us so.

Nikos Kazantzakis described this wholeness sublimely:

Every integral man has inside him, in his heart of hearts, a mystic center around which all else revolves. . . . For some this center is love, for others kindness or beauty, others the thirst for knowledge or the longing for gold and power. They examine the relative value of all else and subordinate it to this central passion. Alas, for the man who does not feel himself governed inside by an absolute monarch. His ungoverned, incoherent life is scattered to the four winds.[13]

For the believer, that passion (or strongest desire) is to reflect the presence of God in his or her very person. For me personally, passion is felt in the journey itself, because throughout the adventure of living I've experienced his sturdy hand holding me and directing me. He has consistently proven himself faithful, and because of this I try to look at everything through the lens of his presence in my life. He's my "absolute Monarch," my "mystic center."

The apostle Paul said the same thing in Colossians 1:27: "The mystery in a nutshell is just this: Christ is in you, therefore you can look forward to sharing in God's glory. It's that simple. That is the substance of our Message" (MSG). When I take that verse at face value and begin to examine what it says in everyday terms, it's mind-boggling to me that Jesus Christ lives in me. What a concept. The fact that he chooses to commingle with me in this way is unfathomable! The truth that I can be integrated and whole in him both challenges and delights me.

Jesus reflects the perfect balance between knowing the truth and living from the heart. Jesus has neither a sterile, academic approach to life, nor an undue emphasis on emotionalism. He brings together our heads and our hearts to make us soulish persons who reflect the harmony of grace and truth, just as he did when he was on this earth. He gives us the will to walk according to his way. By living in us, he provides the balance we need for a full life in both camps—thinking and feeling. And he enables us to make good choices.

For me, there are three areas where I see and experience his unique governing in my life in revolutionary ways: prayer, community, and stewardship. And in each there is very real opportunity to experience exhilarating adventure.

PRAYER

Prayer has been one of the sweetest adventures of my life. I believe with all my heart that prayer really does change things.

Prayer also changes me. As I praise him, my burdens lift. The burdens themselves may not change, but they're transferred from my shoulders to God's. As I unload my cares on him, I sense his presence and strengthening. As I confess my sin and wrong attitudes, I know he forgives me. Since he lives in me, geographically that transfer is done in a matter of seconds—if I can just remember that.

There's a wonderful old poem by John Donne where he confesses his sin then receives the Lord's forgiveness. I've memorized this poem and say it when my heart is especially heavy:

> Wilt thou forgive that sinne where I begunne,
> Which is my sin, though it were done before?
> Wilt thou forgive those sinnes, through which I runne,
> And do run still: though still I do deplore?
> When thou hast done, thou hast not done,
> For I have more.
>
> Wilt thou forgive that sinne by which I have wonne
> Others to sinne? And, made my sinne their doore?
> Wilt thou forgive that sinne which I did shunne
> A yeare, or two: but wallowed in, a score?

When thou hast done, thou hast not done,
For I have more.

I have a sinne of feare, that when I have spunne
My last thred, I shall perish on the shore;
Sweare by thy selfe, that at my death thy sonne
Shall shine as he shines now, and heretofore;
And having done that, Thou hast done,
I feare no more.[14]

In spite of the fact nobody knows exactly what John Donne was referring to in his own life when he wrote those agonizing words, there is something in the poem that speaks to me. It assures me that no matter how heinous or continuous my sin, or how often I bring it to God for forgiveness, he will and does forgive me. I know that in my head, and I experience it in my heart. This kind of prayer helps me "go in peace" afterward.

Sometimes the hurt and pain of the heart are so deep that one can do nothing more than groan or cry out. There are no words to capture the anguish. Fortunately for us, "the Spirit helps us in our weakness. We do not know what we ought to pray for, but the Spirit himself intercedes for us with groans that words cannot express" (Romans 8:26). The primal heart cry of prayer is invaluable. It cleanses us and sustains us and gives us strength to go on.

A friend and I had what I consider a sacred moment in Dallas. Knowing I love old buildings, Doris wanted to show me the architectural wonders of the Catholic cathedral in the heart of the city. It was about dusk, and the building was totally empty except for a lone man right down front, audibly pouring his heart out to God. Kneeling and crying as though his heart would break, he released occasional outbursts of sheer agony. The sun's rays were coming through the stained-glass windows landing on his back, as though they were piercing through his shirt into his body. His very soul was being lacerated.

Without a word, Doris and I looked at each other as if to say, "We have walked into the private sanctuary of someone's pain. We have to leave." And we did.

I will never forget that moment, or that man, or how that made me feel. It was happening outside my body, yet I felt it deep within. It was the cry of all lowly humanity calling out to the heights of divinity for help and comfort.

There is no escaping the undeniable fact that we need an advocate to go before us as well as run with us. Someone who will fight our battles and cheer us on. Someone who will renew us and strengthen us for the next task. This person is the Savior, Jesus Christ, God and man in one person forever. This hypostatic unity of undiminished deity and true humanity enables him to know my need, receive my burden, heal my wound, and send me on my way with his blessing and power. Not only that, but it enables me to experience his love, forgiveness, and solace because he knows my longing heart so intimately.

First Peter 5:6–7 tells us the power of his promise: "Humble yourselves, therefore, under God's mighty hand, that he may lift you up in due time. Cast all your anxiety on him because he cares for you." At the moment we cast our anxiety on our heavenly Father, believing he'll listen, understand, care, and act on our behalf, our burden is lifted. Believing he truly cares is worth a fortune in hope, victory, and spiritual rest. And knowing he is able to respond to our need is a comfort beyond all measure. I know he can do anything, and I feel safe and carefully tended, knowing he will accomplish what concerns me. These precious truths are in my head, and they have become priceless treasures buried deeply in my heart.

COMMUNITY

As far back as I can remember, I've had sweet fellowship and a sense of community with my family and friends. We often talk about spiritual things and the importance of a relationship with God. I well remember my parents praying together about financial concerns, health issues, and various family problems. Because of this kind of vulnerability in my earliest community, I've always sought out relationships in which I can be real and honest. I don't want anybody to judge me; I want to be myself and know that is okay.

One of the reasons I love working with Women of Faith is the loyalty I feel among this fantastic team of friends whom I deeply love and respect—especially Marilyn Meberg, Sheila Walsh, and Patsy Clairmont (who have been here as long as I have). I also have to add Mary Graham (the president) and Nicole Johnson (the dramatist). They don't censure or criticize me. They make me laugh and think and feel and want more and more time with them. For the most part, they consistently model the way I want to be. The fact that they came along at this juncture in my life is almost too good to be true. It is an enormous gift of grace from the Lord, and I never take it for granted.

When we meet each weekend in another city, another venue, another hotel, I feel the same strong bond. I don't have to earn their love. They don't dump their problems on me, expecting me to make them feel better or fill some empty spot inside them. They accept me for exactly who I am, and I do the same with them. We respect each other's personal boundaries and differences. The six of us share confidences that are kept within the confines of our community, and we fight for one another when someone

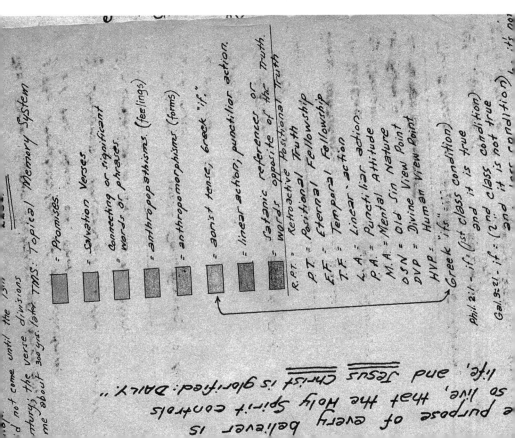

threatens our harmony or unity. I'm not saying we don't have occasional conflicts or don't have to work through problems from time to time. But this unique grouping of Porch Pals gives rise to a sweetness I've never quite known before. The five sisters I never had! They are marvelous friends, and I'm proud and grateful to be working with each of them.

I've often thought that this is the kind of community I've yearned for all along my life's journey—one in which there is boundless love, extravagant grace, and outrageous joy. We all give and we all receive; we care and we're cared for; we're in it for the long haul. The sweet fellowship we enjoy is born out of knowing that God is using all of us no matter how we got to this place. Ephesians 2:19 says, "God is building a home. He's using us all— irrespective of how we got here—in what he is building" (MSG). For that awe-inspiring and joy-producing truth, we praise him. None of us anticipated this leg of our journey. We simply signed on to do a job—we had no idea God would change our lives.

Nothing I experienced in my childhood was as good as this. Nothing in the way of personal or career accomplishment was as good as this. The hours of work may be long and the way tiring, but I wouldn't trade this season of life for anything. I'm on an adventure, wherever it takes me, and my heart is overflowing with the goodness that comes from him all along the way. Nothing in any foreign port or countryside is as beautiful as the face of the person who knows Christ as Savior, who lives from his or her "mystic center"—and I have the profound privilege and joy of living in spiritual community with a band of troubadours who do just that.

STEWARDSHIP

The basic principle behind being a good steward is the genuine belief that we are richer than we think. Because of this, our giving becomes greater than we believe to be prudent, since our source of wealth is inexhaustible. That's a mouthful, I know, but living out of that endowment is what makes us capable of being generous from the heart.

Stewardship is a practice that goes beyond managing our material possessions; I understand it also to include time and energy—anything that is ours to spend. When we share out of the fullness of our being, out of a spirit of openness and flexibility, we are truly rich. We experience a vitality that comes from an inner source.

I used to tithe faithfully when I was growing up, out of my little allowance. It seemed easy and right and obedient to what I was taught by my parents and what they modeled. But when I got out on my own and made my own living, I never felt I had enough money. I always thought I'd run out. Isn't that something? Have a little—tithe. Have a lot—can't. Go figure! As I looked at the circumstances of my life, I made what seemed like a reasonable decision. There was never any extra money, so how could I give? I didn't. I neglected to look at my situation from God's perspective. And my logic was leading me astray.

One day when I was sufficiently convicted about this and the guilt was naggingly troublesome, I talked with my brother Chuck about it and asked him what I should do. We chatted a bit about the scriptural references to tithing, beginning way back in Genesis 14:20 where Abram gave the priest a tenth of everything he had. Academically, I understood the principle involved and agreed wholeheartedly.

As I remember, the conversation with Chuck went something like this:

"Why don't you tithe, Sis? You can't outdo God. It's not possible."

"Well . . . I don't know. I guess I feel I'll run out of money before I run out of month. It's that simple. I don't have enough to go around."

"Why don't you try it? Just try it for a while and see what happens. God will prove himself faithful; you'll see."

"You mean tithe even before I get out of debt?"

"Yes. Even before that. You may never get out of debt."

Sigh.

"But what if I run out?"

"You won't. But, if you do, come see me. I'll help you." (He knew God wouldn't let that happen, and deep inside, I knew it, too.)

"Oh, and don't start with ten percent, Sis. Anybody can give ten percent. Start higher."

"How 'bout eleven?"

"Eleven is good. You'll see. Just start and watch how God works in the smallest ways. He'll meet all your needs when you become a good steward of your finances. One more thing, Sis: Always tithe off the gross, not the net. Everything, everything you make, from top to bottom, belongs to the Lord, not to you. Remember it's just on loan to you anyway."

And so it began. First, I told God I was sorry I had neglected this very direct instruction for so many years, and I wanted to change that right away. I asked him to show me a good percentage to start with, and that I'd be at peace with that figure until he told me otherwise. As always with the God of grace, I felt no condemnation, no scolding or ridicule coming back from him. I felt no need to chastise myself for the years I'd wandered in error. He met me right where I was. And we started right then and there, as if I'd never done it wrong.

I tithed eleven percent for four years or so, and then I decided twelve percent was better. Then thirteen. Then fifteen. On and on. And, I always tithe off the gross, just like Chuck said, and I have never gone wanting in all these years. In fact, I've been far more financially secure than I ever was before. God continually proves himself faithful in the area of supplying my needs. I had no way of being certain that would happen, but the scriptural principle proved true.

Os Guinness says, "We don't give, because it all belongs to the Lord anyway. . . . We give because we've been given to." When we look at ourselves as the constant recipients of the continual grace and goodness of God, our generous Father, how can we overdo in giving to others? He is our inexhaustible source. I especially like a comment by Dr. Stephen Olford: "God demands our tithes; he delights in our offerings. When we do that he defends our savings and defrays our expenses."

One of the greatest adventures as God's children is trusting our Father with respect to our finances, our time, and our energy. Giving from our wealth—no matter how small or large—is not even a gamble, although we're dealing with the great unknown because of our own limited vision. But God has promised to meet our needs, and he won't go back on his promise.

Giving freely of the resources God has given me has become downright enjoyable. I figure if he can turn water into wine, he can provide riches out of nowhere. He's got the goods to do it! I could recount story after story of his surprises to me in terms of replenishing my well of money, time, and energy. His bounteous goodness constantly rains on my parade.

I also find in the matter of giving that the greater the trust, the wider the blessing. And the wider the blessing, the sweeter the joy. I couldn't have made those statements forty years ago, or maybe even twenty, when I wasn't as free in my spirit as I am now. But I've learned from personal experience that God keeps his word and continually gives out of a well that never runs dry. Chuck was right. Nobody can outdo God.

Second Corinthians 8:9 teaches, "For you know the grace of our Lord Jesus Christ, that though he was rich, yet for your sakes he became poor, so that you through his poverty might become rich." In light of such heartfelt grace, how can any of us not be generous? When I look at stewardship through the lens of Scripture, I am abundantly rich and can afford to give away everything I have. His grace has made me a millionaire.

So many people are fragmented. Their lives are broken and splintered. They don't know who they are and can't figure out why they're here. Their lives contain very little joy and no sense of adventure. But what Christ offers us, today and every day of our lives, is just the opposite. We're given wholeness because we are centered on him who is the center of the universe. Through prayer, we have constant communion with him. In fellowship with others we enjoy community that gratifies. And through the stewardship of our borrowed resources, we have something tangible to contribute to others. Christ is our solid center, our absolute Monarch, and in him we think and move and feel and have our being.

God has promised to meet our needs, and he can't go back on that promise.
Start an ongoing list of all the specific ways God meets your needs.

_____

_____

_____

_____

_____

_____

_____

_____

_____

_____

_____

_____

_____

_____

_____

_____

_____

_____

_____

_____

_____

Prayer changes us. As we praise God, our burdens lift. As we unload our cares on him, we sense his presence and strengthening. As we confess our sins and wrong attitudes, he forgives us and gives us peace.

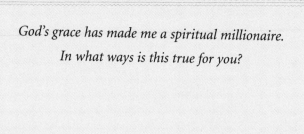

God's grace has made me a spiritual millionaire.

In what ways is this true for you?

We make a living by what we get—we make a life by what we give.

—Winston Churchill

_____

_____

_____

_____

_____

_____

_____

_____

_____

_____

_____

_____

_____

_____

_____

_____

_____

_____

_____

_____

In 1994 I invested a chunk o' change in a nice telescope and couldn't wait to get home with it. It was late October when that big, full autumn moon fills the sky and the heavens are alive with stars. You know the season.

I carefully read all the instructions, figured out what to do, and put it together. Night came, and I set the telescope in front of the picture window in my dining room, working with the lens dial to focus on the moon, hanging up there waiting for me to have a look.

Nothing happened. I couldn't see a thing.

I pulled out the directions again and reread them—went through all the steps, double-checked each item, and set it back up. Again, nothing. I was getting discouraged, so I decided to call it quits, have a Snickers, go to bed, and try again tomorrow night. (A Snickers is always a good reward for effort and comfort food when things don't go well.)

Next night. Another full, luminescent moon. Gorgeous. I couldn't wait. But the telescope wouldn't work. *What is wrong with this idiotic thing?* I simply could not focus the lens. "All I want to do is see something in the distance," I told the telescope. What am I doing wrong here? For over an hour I fiddled with the lens, tripod, dial, adjusting this and that, and I finally caught a quick glimpse of the moon, like a shadow . . . hazy, oblique. Dissatisfied, I put the telescope away.

A few days later I took my disappointing purchase back to the store and got another one. I started again at square one. I fiddled and adjusted some more. After working with it off and on for literally weeks but never seeing much of anything, I finally ran out of time and patience and put it in the bottom of the closet.

Maybe I try too hard to see what's in the distance with everything. I catch just enough glimpses of beauty to know I will love it when it comes into clear focus, but then it never quite does. There's only a hazy image of the real thing. And I go away disappointed, wondering.

Some aspects of my spiritual life are like that, too. I wonder what's in the distance, over that hill, down the road, around the corner, beyond today. What kind of adventure does God have for me next? Will it be hard or easy? Will I recognize it's from him? God has left a lot unsaid in the areas where I want to know more, and no matter what I do, I can't figure it out. It's simply not for me to know.

My daddy's favorite Bible verse was 1 Corinthians 2:9, "No eye has seen, no ear has heard, no mind has conceived what God has prepared for those who love him." He quoted it many times to me, wrote it in letters, and jotted it on gift cards. It makes me wonder if he, too, wondered what was in the distance, over life's horizon. Now he knows, of course, since he's been in the presence of the Lord for more than thirty years. He knows, even as he is known.

Gratefully, my own ultimate tomorrow is a given as well. When I put my faith in Jesus Christ as my Savior, I sealed my destiny. The finished work of Christ and his promise about what is to come assures me I'll spend eternity with him. God has made it clear in his Word that someday he will come get me and take me to live with him forever.

Frankly, I love the fact that God has a plan for the future, for every tomorrow of my life on earth and beyond. Even though I can't figure it all out, he's got it wired. This reassures me that I'm loved and safe. "There is a future for the man of peace," David tells us in Psalm 37:37. And Jeremiah 29:11 assures us, "'For I know the plans I have for you,' declares the LORD, 'plans to prosper you and not to harm you, plans to give you hope and a future.'" God knows our course and he knows us. He loves us. He provides. He plans ahead.

Because the Lord has set this example, I firmly believe I need to plan ahead as well—to consider the tomorrows of my life while still living fully in today. I want tomorrow to be adventuresome, certainly, but I'd also like to avoid as many unpleasant surprises as possible. There is absolutely no way I can know what will happen, but if the future is like the past, then it will surely come, and I need to think ahead and be ready. To the degree I'm able, I sincerely want to be ready. I believe the Lord will take care of me throughout the course of my life, but I would also like to take care of myself as long as possible, in whatever ways will enhance my physical, mental, and spiritual health.

In the early '90s I engaged the services of mental health professionals and went to them for private counseling sessions. It was a very positive experience in the long run, although there were moments (for one reason or another) I wanted to storm out of the session screaming and drive like a maniac back to my house. Or better yet, kill the therapist.

In that eighteen-month span of time, I had two counselors, a man and a woman, and they each did me a world of good. On the poor woman I dumped every negative thing I had ever thought about any human being who ever crossed my path, thus getting it out of my system. And with the man I began to pick up the scattered debris that was left of my inner life and put it back together.

There's something very gratifying and healing to one's soul about dumping the truck then rifling through the trash pile, deciding what's important to keep and throwing the rest away. It's sort of a "come to Jesus" moment, as my friend Marilyn calls it—an important, defining time in one's personal growth. When I started to put the pieces back together, I made a list of five things I really wanted out of life from then on—through all my tomorrows.

A RICH, MEANINGFUL RELATIONSHIP WITH THE LORD

Because I believe God has a plan for my life, both temporally and eternally, I want to live in a way that will please him. I may not always know what that is, but I generally know what it's not. It's my responsibility to strike out in faith, believing he will show me as I go along. God holds the future of my life. I feel secure in the fact that the blood of his Son was shed for my sins and because of that fact I will spend eternity in heaven. With this as a given, I want my activities on earth to count for him. I want to invest time in active fellowship with Jesus, because I believe that the closer I am to God the better my life will go, even in its worst moments. "The Lord is my Shepherd; I shall not want." The "Shepherd" part is doctrine, a given on which I can count. The "wanting" part is a feeling, on which I can't count. It is always my desire to live out of the doctrinal part of that verse; thus I know all my wants will be met in him. This goes for today, tomorrow, and forever!

A SENSE OF HOMEOSTASIS WHEREVER I AM IN THE WORLD

Since this world is not my home and I am a sojourner and pilgrim on my way to heaven, I hope to get as much out of this place as possible, in terms of travel. I'd like to go everywhere. The future is an open book, and the parameters are only in my mind. As my daddy said years ago, "You can go anywhere, do anything . . . just line your will up with the will of God and go."

I want to be a citizen of the world, not just Texas or California or the USA. I'd like my heart to reach out to all kinds of people, cultures, and ideas. It doesn't mean I will embrace or believe everything I encounter, but I do want to know about it and feel comfortable learning. Hermann Hesse said in his existential novel *Demian*, "Where paths that have affinity for each other intersect, the whole world looks like home, for a time." I have found that statement to be so true. I'd like to feel that intersection whether I'm on home turf or foreign soil. Anywhere in the world. All the time.

I love these lines by Charles Swain, a nineteenth-century poet:

> Home's not merely four square walls,
> Though with pictures hung and gilded;
> Home is where affection calls,—
> Filled with shrines the heart hath builded.

It may not be perfect grammar, but it's a mouthful of truth.

ENOUGH MONEY TO MEET MY NEEDS

When I left Mobil Oil Corporation, I was fully vested in their retirement fund. With the help of an excellent financial planner, I invested carefully. In these investments lie my financial future. I've also prepared a will delineating to whom my assets will go.

I truly believe it is right to keep one's house "in order." Realistically speaking it's not possible to do that all the time, but I think we should work at it. It helped enormously to hire this financial guy. When I have a question, I turn to him, and he has shepherded me through the ups and downs of the stock market. He's given me expert counsel, always leaving the final decision up to me. I like that. I want it that way. But, even with wise counsel, I don't always know what to do. So I pray, and I wait. In time, the answer comes, and I've learned to trust that answer. It may not be perfect, but it's good enough to act on.

The older I get, the less speedily I make decisions. Especially big ones. Being Texan, my decisions weren't ever up to speed anyway, but they do reflect a lot of deliberation and thought. Right or wrong, this works for me. I may not think long about buying a book, but I do think long about investing in pork bellies.

Money is my medium of exchange, and when I'm old and gray(er), I'd like to have something to exchange. So I'm pretty cautious.

CONTENTMENT IN ALL CIRCUMSTANCES

Oh boy. This is the hardest one on the list when I think of the future. Let's say something happened where I lost my health and was no longer able to function independently. Could I learn to be content? Good question. The answer lies in the word *learn*. Of course that would be very difficult for me—one who has known independence my entire adult life. But I know the apostle Paul said he learned to be content in all circumstances (Philippians 4:12). Learning to be content is an educational process, as is all learning. It takes time, and I'm sure over time at least some measure of contentment would come. It would start with the acceptance of present reality and hopefully move toward genuine contentment.

Funny thing, but when I told my therapist about this desire on my list, he smiled and said quietly, "Fat chance." How true. How in the world can I be content in all circumstances? I really don't believe I can, but I'll try. I'll throw my heart into it and ask the Lord for his help. Hardships, losses, inconveniences, interruptions, relinquishments—I could name twenty things I have to work at to find contentment. Maybe it won't happen in some arenas. I don't know. I do know one thing: If I don't want it, it will never come. Never even be a blip on the horizon. I call God into these dark areas of my life all the time, asking him to illumine me with his wisdom and encouragement, then help me follow him into the light.

AN ABIDING KNOWLEDGE THAT MY LIFE HAS PURPOSE

I want a reason to get up in the morning. When I ask God for a sense of personal destiny, and then listen carefully, I get a sense of direction. Not always, and not always immediately, but I rely on God's promise to consistently guide me toward fulfilling the purpose for which he created me. Proverbs 16:9 reminds us, "In his heart a man plans his course, but the LORD determines his steps." And verse 3 promises, "Commit to the Lord whatever you do, and your plans will succeed." Love that!

Each time I stand on the Women of Faith stage and see those thousands of faces in the audience, I am totally amazed that I'm standing up there. Why me? Because I asked for purpose? Because God wants to use me for such a time as this? Maybe. But I don't know for sure. All I'm certain of is that nothing any of us experiences is pointless or useless. The good, the bad, the ugly, even the things we think will kill us—God uses it all, and he devises our destiny out of the stuff in our trash. He sifts it out, shows us the value, and then uses us to help others because of it. We all meet in our humanity.

When we look at the desires of our hearts in light of reality, we know none of them is achievable all the time. They're changeable, like the weather. Some days we're content; others we're not. There are places in the world we feel completely at home, others less so. There are even days when we wonder if we have a purpose at all, and the uncertainty lingers for a while. But our desires give shape and substance to our unique essences. And when we pray out of the depth of those desires, our faith is strengthened and our fellowship with the Lord is sweeter.

🐚

I was reading from the *Living Insights Bible* not long ago and ran across something my brother Chuck said about the future, about being ready for the return of Christ—our ultimate tomorrow.

Remember the watchwords: occupy, purify, watch and worship. If you're engaged in those four things, you won't have to get ready; you'll be ready! No need to try to set a date or quit your job or dress up in a white robe. Just live every day as if it were the last. You'll be surprised at the difference it'll make in how you think, how you respond . . . how you live![15]

You got that right, Bro. In fact, I have a letter from Chuck written December 16, 1957, that says almost the same thing. He was a marine, preparing to be shipped to the island of Okinawa. He wrote me dozens of letters during those two years of service in the military, and I've kept them all. In this particular letter his closing paragraph reads:

He's a wonderful Savior but best of all—He loves even me. Praise His name! I'm ready for His return. In fact, I stay ready to keep from getting ready. I must close before my heart leaps from my chest!

We love our sis, Cynthia and Babe

Get this—Amen and Amen!!!
"Thou drewest near in the day that I called upon Thee: Thou Saidst, Fear Not" (Lamentations 3:57).

How 'bout that?

The very best way to face tomorrow is to Fear Not. "Stay ready to keep from getting ready." I love that phrase! We know who holds all our tomorrows. He's coming to get us, then we're outta here. We won't even have to change clothes.

God knows. He loves.
He plans ahead.

I want to be a citizen of the world, not just Texas or California or the USA.

I'd like my heart to reach out to all kinds of people, cultures, and ideas.

It doesn't mean I will embrace or believe everything I encounter,

but I do want to know about it and feel comfortable learning.

Allow God's incorruptible truth to become the protoplasm of your soul.
Without doubt he will make a way for you to be truly yourself—
apart from having anybody else in your life. You will grow
in him when you rely on what he says.

_____

_____

_____

_____

_____

_____

_____

_____

_____

_____

_____

_____

_____

_____

_____

_____

_____

_____

_____

If your faith doesn't work when the chips are down
and you never use it . . . what good is it anyway?
—Florence Bergendahl

NIKON NUVIS
W/ZOOM LENS...
22.5-66mm

PART 5

CAPTURING THE POSSIBILITIES

PART 5

In 1989 I had a flip calendar that was nothing but questions. Three hundred and sixty-five questions. Some of them were easy to answer, others were hard, but all were hypothetical and fun to consider. Each day I set about applying my best judgment to figure out an answer as if my life depended on it. In the course of that year, I learned things about myself I hadn't known before:

Q. Would you rather be extremely successful in an unconventional way few people could relate to or in a conventional way people could identify with more easily?

A. In an unconventional way. I prefer to be the one who goes out on a limb to succeed. It makes life more interesting.

Q. If an eccentric millionaire arranged a surprise party for you that would be attended by everyone you had ever known and you found out about it a few hours before it was to start, would you be filled more with eagerness or dread?

A. Eagerness! I would love to be at such a party . . . especially if it were a surprise and money was no object. I could die after that, knowing I had touched base with everyone in my life I'd ever known.

Q. Would you be willing to endure four months of isolation on a small rocky island if you knew you would not only survive the difficult experience but would come away from it with an unwavering core of self-confidence and spiritual awareness?

A. No. I'd rather have two weeks in the Ritz-Carlton in Paris. I can find self-confidence and spiritual awareness in easier ways.

Q. If somehow you could save a thousand people from death by causing the complete eradication of a great work of literature, for example, *Hamlet,* would you do so?

A. Depends on the people.

Q. If you could have all your needs and desires met, do you think you would still have stress in your life?

A. Absolutely. It's not possible to get rid of stress totally as long as I'm in the human condition.

These kinds of questions are playful as well as self-revealing. They provide enjoyment, but they also give us pause. While tickling our cerebral funny bones, they make us think—and we generally become what we think about.

The ability to think is a wonderful gift. We take it for granted, yet what would it be like if we couldn't remember, evaluate, determine, make plans,

A much younger Luci . . . in my guitar-playing days.

Forest Hills

on leave now at 6611 99th St., F
Hills, L. I.

decide right from wrong, or change our minds? When I ask myself hypothetical questions—"If I had the chance, would I do that again?" "Could I learn to fly a hot air balloon?" "Should I have been a mud wrestler?"—in effect I reestablish who I am and validate the fact that it's okay to be me. I've done this kind of thing all my life at various stages. The mind is like a compass, and I want mine set at true north. After all,

> Christ is not the end, He is the beginning. He is not the "Welcome!" He
> is the "Bon Voyage!" He does not sit back restfully in soft clouds, but is
> battered by the waves just as we are, His eyes fixed aloft on the North
> Star, His Hands firmly on the helm.[16]

It has been said that sixty-five thousand thoughts float through our minds each day. Every one of those thoughts has the seed of possibility in it. We choose with our will what we'll do with that thought. Will we stay stuck in "If only . . ." or "Why me?"—or will we open our minds to "What if?" and "Why not?"

Let's never stop asking questions. Questions give us a harbor to remember where we once lived mentally. They remind us of the possibilities that can be born out of thoughts and musings, and they link together patterns that define our lives. Asking questions keeps us open-minded and openhearted to what was and is and might be in the years to come. They send us on our way into all sorts of journeys in search of adventure.

How many more years do I have on this earth? (Now, there's a question I ponder a lot.) Only the Lord knows. Being a spiritual sojourner, I know I'm on my way to a better place anyway, but now seems like a good time to pause and look back. I want to assess where I've come from and where I'm going—I want to ask myself what things I'd do the same, might do differently, or regret I never did at all.

Want to come with me? I invite you to make your own list as we go along. We'll both see how the possibilities never end. We can do all things through Christ. His is the hand that launches us; his Spirit propels us. The voyage doesn't get any better than that.

Several years ago I was invited to speak at an ecumenical, nondenominational study group sponsored by a Congregational church in Greenwich, Connecticut. The meeting, including a luncheon, was held at the Greenwich Country Club and was open to the public. About three hundred women were in attendance . . . all perfectly groomed, beautifully dressed, and absolutely charming. I loved it!

During lunch, I sat next to a darling young woman who worked at the New York Stock Exchange. We struck up a fun conversation about money, investments, stocks and bonds, capital gains, and so forth. I mostly listened as she told story after story of what it was like working there. She and her husband were business partners. I found that fascinating.

"Do you and he ever compare notes?" I asked.

"Yes, sometimes," she said. "But I don't really trust his judgment about money."

I was amused. "You don't?"

"No. You see, my husband's a wonderful man, but he and I think so differently." Then she launched into how she'd gotten a reliable tip on a particular stock a few months back that was going to go big, and she asked for her husband's advice. He discouraged her from buying it and said that the information was all wet. She shouldn't do it. Turns out she took his advice and the stock went through the roof. Made a killing.

"I could have been a millionaire today if I'd done what my heart told me to do," she said, "but I didn't. I really regret that."

"Regret not being a millionaire?" I asked.

"No. Regret telling my husband . . . I should've followed my heart!"

Everybody has regrets. Some are small, some large, but it's impossible to go through life without collecting at least a few.

In looking back now, I see some areas where I wish I had followed my heart too. I'm not saying I can't do these things now, but they're not as easy as when I was younger. If I had struck while the iron was hot, I think I'd be a better person for it. A richer person with a kinder, gentler spirit. I also think had I done these things differently at an earlier age, my life would be of more benefit to others now.

Probably none of what I list is hugely significant to anybody but me, but reviewing our regrets can actually be worthwhile. Who knows, it might not even be too late to cross some of them off our lists. So, if I had my life to live over, I would at least consider doing these things differently:

GET MORE FORMAL EDUCATION

The enjoyment of learning has been such a passion of mine; I've often wished I had a master's degree, or even a doctorate. I know it would have taken a great deal of effort, discipline, and dedication, but I've wondered why I didn't bite that off to chew as a young adult. Some people go back to school as senior citizens, but not without giving up at least a portion of their current lives. I'm not so sure I could accomplish this now if I wanted to, simply because my mind isn't as sharp as it once was.

With reading and traveling I've done my best to keep up with educating myself beyond an undergraduate level, but it would have been fun to have another degree under my belt just for the sheer joy of learning. Maybe I'll do that when I'm not running around the country with Women of Faith. It's always in the back of my mind.

HAVE A PET

That sentence looks strange to me. Is that the way I want to put it? I started to write, "Own a pet," but one really doesn't own anything that already has a life. Every one of my closest friends has a pet—a dog or cat or horse or goldfish or something that is dependent upon someone for its care—and in some cases they have more than one of each. But somehow

this kind of responsibility has never appealed to me. I regret that. I've become fascinated with wild animals in Africa, so I've wondered how that can be. I can't quite figure it out. When I was growing up, both of my brothers had dogs, and my dearest girlhood friend had a cat. (Actually, the cat had her, which is the case with all "cat people," I'm told.) I had neither and, I'm sad to say, never wanted an animal.

It makes me chastise myself in a way; I view myself as somewhat cold-hearted. I don't think I wanted the responsibility, but had I had the responsibility, I think I would have become a softer person, more generous in my spirit toward all creatures because that is the way all my animal-loving friends are. This may be a silly thing to confess, but as I think back, I do believe I would do this differently.

The only roommate I ever had raised Chihuahuas. In fact, she had several. The most adorable was Bonnie, who actually won best in show in a Dallas dog show. She was darling. As Bonnie grew older and became frailer, she stopped eating and began lying in her little bed from morning till night. One evening I came home from the office and found her dead on the floor a foot or two from her bed. I cried and cried. For some reason, the loss of Bonnie affected me so deeply I didn't think I would recover. I was depressed for weeks. The ironic part was that my roommate's grief was not nearly as long or severe as mine.

Maybe that's why I never had an animal of my own. Perhaps I don't trust my emotions. Perhaps I fear that loving an animal would make me too vulnerable. I just wish I had done that differently a long time ago.

I have thought recently that if I didn't travel so much I'd get two cats . . . name them Here and Now. If Here was there when I wanted her to be with me, maybe Now would be here. Just a thought.

LEARN OTHER LANGUAGES

My wonderful Greek friend, Sophia, who was born in Athens and lived there all her life, speaks five languages fluently—Greek, English, French, Italian, and German. I marvel at this. Had she not spoken English, in fact, we would not be friends today.

I was shopping with Sophia on the island of Mykonos once, and the proprietor was the only salesperson there to help customers. As she and Sophia were chatting, a crowd of shoppers of every nationality under the sun descended upon the place from a cruise ship that had just pulled into the harbor. The shop owner looked stricken. She said to Sophia (in Greek, of course), "What am I going to do? I don't know what they're saying." Without hesitation, Sophia stepped right in, and I watched as she kindly took care of every customer in his or her own language. It was thrilling to witness.

I studied Spanish and German in college and a bit of Italian while singing professionally. I know a few French words and have a pretty good facility for pronunciation, but I would give anything to be fluent in any one of these languages. I think it'd be fun to read, write, and speak a language other than my mother tongue. I wish I had followed my heart earlier in that and taken classes, as I intended to. I regret putting it off.

LIVE IN EUROPE

This desire is related to the last one. I've often thought how enjoyable it would have been to live in Paris and study languages at the Sorbonne; or Florence and study art at the Uffizi Gallery; or Vienna and study international law at the University. This is the stuff my dreams are made of. As a senior in college, I applied for a Fulbright scholarship but wasn't accepted, so I began working for Mobil Oil Corporation, with the thought I'd be there a year then go back for a master's degree. And you know that story.

Judy Jacobs, my friend who lived in Rome two years after she graduated from Southern Methodist University in Dallas, is one of the most interesting persons I know. She speaks fluent Italian and was the translator for our Italian maestro when I sang with the Dallas Civic Opera chorus. Her parents offered her the gift of foreign travel upon college graduation, and once she got to Europe, she loved it so much she decided to stay. She found a job as a governess with the family of a medical doctor in Rome, phoned home to tell her parents, and started living there. Because the family for whom she worked was wealthy, she traveled with them to St. Moritz. She shopped in Paris and New York and, of course, traveled all over Italy. She has told me it was an adventure of a lifetime. I'll bet.

This wonderful early experience opened an enormous door for Judy with respect to all manner of travel. Since those days, she's seen the world and is still hopping planes and ships, always with the next excursion in mind. In the last four years, Judy has sent me postcards from Asia, Scandinavia, and Antartica. You go, girl!

I'm told that little can compare to living in another country. If I were in my twenties or thirties, you can bet your bottom dollar that is one thing I would do—for sure. No question about following my heart on this one.

PLAY THE PIANO

If there were lots of time in my future, this would be a must for me. I'd love to tickle the ivories! My grandmother and mother both played and taught as far back as I can remember. And they were good. My older brother plays and so do his children. And they are good. I horse around but don't play, and I am bad. I love the sound of a piano . . . all those chords and nuances. Fingers are dancing in my head right now.

It would be fun after a hard day at work to sit down at the keyboard, play and sing, and have a good old time with music. Imagine a gathering that's kind of quiet or boring and somebody hops up, goes to the piano, and starts playing. Suddenly everybody's spirits lift, and there's music in the air. People start singing and dancing. We think of a dozen songs right off the bat that we all know. We feel better because the music soothes our troubled souls. I'd like to be the one to do that for everybody. Call out a tune, any tune. I can play it!

I do play the ukulele and a bit of guitar, which are both enjoyable, fun instruments, but the piano offers a lot more variety. If a little genie said right now, "You can play any instrument you want; name it and at the snap of my fingers you'll be doing it," I'd choose the piano, hands down.

TEACH ART HISTORY

One of my favorite pastimes is visiting art museums. There is a sense of permanence about museums of any kind, but art museums are the best in my estimation. You've got your history and your beauty, all rolled into one. And, to teach others to love them as much as I do would be wonderful. I wish I had started taking friends to museums when I was in high school. For the past twenty or thirty years I've done that, but if I'd started sooner, I'd know more, they'd know more, and everybody would have benefited.

I did teach a little art class in my home in the '60s when I lived in Dallas. There were only a handful of folks who came, but oh, the fun we had. Sunday afternoon, after church, we'd get together and read one of John Canaday's *Seminars in Art Portfolios* from the Metropolitan Museum of Art. Old books, but a wonderful source of information. We went together to a couple of museums and learned lots of things about the beauty of paintings and sculpture. We all began looking at life in a deeper, richer way. Why didn't I keep that up? With my degree in art, I often wish I had been an art instructor, especially for adults who love to learn and haven't been exposed to this boundless area of beauty. It's not that I know so much; it's that we could all be learning together, and that would be the fun of it. Rats! I'm mad right now that I didn't do that!

A few years ago I was enjoying casual conversation with friends as we were traveling by train in Great Britain. I asked if they could identify their greatest regret in life. After thinking a long while, my charming friend Ney Bailey said, with the consummate sincerity that so characterizes her nature, "I wish I would have taken a really good writing class." The rest of us looked at her for a few seconds then roared with laughter. After the initial shock, Ney joined us. It struck us all so funny because it certainly wasn't too late for her to take that really good writing class. If that is her greatest regret in life, she is one child of fortune.

The truth is that many of life's regrets are reversible. Sometimes what we wish we'd done when we were younger or in different circumstances, we can still pursue. And even mistakes that loom in our history like savage beasts don't have to define us or devour us.

One of my closest friends had two abortions when she was young and tender and misguided. The guilt and shame of those experiences were critical to bringing her to faith in Christ many years ago. Today she has the most vital ministry to young women of anyone I know, anywhere. And what is the source of that ability to minister to young, tender, and misguided women? Her own horrendous experience. In Romans 8:28, the apostle Paul wrote that all things work together for good to those who love God (and we do) and are called according to his purpose (and we are). Does my friend regret her past? Absolutely. Has it ruined her life? Absolutely not—quite the opposite, in fact. In God's economy, it has been instrumental in helping her know and experience his love and grace. She understands forgiveness in a way few ever will. Those who have been forgiven much, love much (see Luke 7:47). Actually, I've never known anyone who exudes love for the Lord and others more than this dear friend.

We can focus so intently on our regrets that we lose perspective. Of course we've made mistakes. Of course we've done stupid things. Of course we've followed bad advice. But who hasn't? Our regrets don't have to be our undoing. I love the way Howard Shultz, the founder of Starbucks, puts it in his book *Pour Your Heart into It*. He writes, "Success should not be measured in dollars: it's about how you conduct the journey, and how big your heart is at the end of it."[17]

When we start believing anything's possible, regrets turn into challenges, defeats into lessons learned, and heartache into magnanimity. It's all in our outlook—the lens through which we choose to view life. If we're not careful, we'll let disappointment or regret prevent us from celebrating what we have achieved. What a waste! Besides, if we had it all to do over, how do we know we wouldn't do it the same way again? Better to live fully in today and place our hope in the future God has planned for us.

Gotta run—I'm late for my piano lesson.

What is the stuff your dreams are made of?

_____

_____

_____

_____

_____

_____

_____

_____

_____

_____

_____

_____

_____

_____

_____

_____

_____

If you had your life to do over, would you do things differently?

The way to have few regrets is to keep short accounts.

_____

_____

_____

_____

_____

_____

_____

_____

_____

_____

_____

_____

_____

_____

_____

_____

_____

_____

Think about all the ways God has brought you through life—
adventures, straights and narrows, good times and bad—and how
he has continually cared for you. Write about those times.

_____

_____

_____

_____

_____

_____

_____

_____

_____

_____

_____

_____

_____

_____

_____

_____

_____

CHAPTER FOURTEEN *Maybe*
EMBRACING VISION AND DREAMS

Southerners use a phrase I love—"might could." I've used that all my life. My mom asks me if I'll pick up something after school. "Sure, I might could if I leave on time." I ask a college friend if she can drop me off at the library on her way to town. "Might could, girlfriend. Hop in." Even in the Mobil Research Lab in Dallas I heard the term "might could" from some of the brightest PhDs in the world. "We might could get a man to investigate the lunar samples if Washington would provide the funding." Or, "I might could negotiate for better terms and conditions if I knew all the parameters."

"Might could" is one of the most common and useful phrases in my background. It grows right out of my roots. The same is true for any Texan. They'll know what I mean, and we're serious. It's like "fize." "Fize you, I wouldn't do that." "Fize that lawyer, I'd drive a harder bargain." "Fize" and "might could" are right up there with "y'all come," "his-sef," and "shore nuff."

When I first met Marilyn, my English teacher friend, she asked what I meant by "might could."

"Well, Mare . . . it means I might if I wanted to and could if I would, but I'm not sure yet." She laughed, but that's exactly what I meant. And that's what I'm talking about in this chapter: things I might do if I wanted to or could if I would, but I'm not sure yet. That'd be a strong maybe.

We all have a list of maybes. They're rather easy to state because they're often outlandish. If they weren't, I would've put them in either the chapter before or after this one, where my choices are more established and defined. But a few challenging dreams have crossed my mind from time to time, and I don't want to bring this adventure to a close without looking at them for a minute. They might could spark a few dreams of your own. They're things I think about when I give in to wild or off-the-wall imaginations. In the land of maybe, life is looked at through a very wide-angle lens. Anything is possible here; no personal vision is too far out. So hang on to your shorts. I have some pretty wacky maybes.

ENTER THE IDITAROD

There's something about this sled dog race that really piques my interest. One thing is that a woman won it several consecutive years. That tells me right there that a female can do it. I like that. The part of Alaskan terrain that has to be crossed from Anchorage to Nome is pristine and virtually untouched by humanity. I like that. The sled dogs are the highest bred, brightest, best-trained, and most dependable of probably any domestic animal, because one's life totally depends on them. I like that, too.

I also like the fact that the Iditarod was inspired by a 1925 relay to deliver serum for an outbreak of diphtheria. It was so dramatic and heartfelt, it turned into the annual dogsled race we know today, born of a benevolent cause.

The sense of competition is fierce and brings out the best in anyone—not only competition but endurance as well. I'd just like to see if I had that kind of strength in me. I wonder if there's an age limit. If not . . . stay tuned. I just might could try it one day.

BUILD A BOAT

This is no ordinary boat. I want to build it then live on it. I first got the idea from one of the engineers at Mobil who did this very thing. It took him a year to build. Then he moved in and got married, and he and his wife lived there. I thought that sounded so romantic and fun. This couple were devout Christians, and they held Bible study classes on the boat, threw parties, sailed out from the slip on moonlit nights, and spent the night offshore.

Can't you just see it? How beautiful! He used to describe for me the twinkling lights in the harbor and how they looked from the deck of his boat.

MEMORIZE THE CONSTITUTION

Memorizing poetry and quotations has always appealed to me. The brain cells are fertile places to plant information and recall it on days when we need encouragement.

But the Constitution? Well . . . why not? This creative document gives credence to our way of life in this nation, and I'd like to be able to recall it at will to support my patriotic beliefs and remind myself what my forefathers fought and died for. I've learned bits and pieces, but not enough to retain the whole in one fell swoop.

I might could memorize it, but the verdict is still out on that. Maybe so. Maybe not. I just keep seeing myself in my mind's eye, standing up at one of the Women of Faith conferences and surprising everybody by starting my speech with, "We the people of the United States, in Order to form a more perfect Union, establish Justice . . . ," then launching right into the gospel. After all, Christ died for the people of the United States. I might could make it all fit together. I just think it's a cool idea.

BE AN ORGAN DONOR—WHILE I'M STILL KICKIN'

If one of my loved ones needed a kidney, I'd like to be the one to contribute mine. I think. I find this kind of sacrifice to be so overwhelmingly generous in spirit it boggles my mind. I've read stories where mothers have done it for their daughters, or husbands for wives, friends for friends. As I've read about these humane gestures, I'm always moved to tears. But could I do it . . . would I have the courage it takes? I don't know, but it's certainly on my list.

MAKE ALL MY GIFTS

Now, this is huge. With my love of figuring things out and having creative activities going on all the time plus the joy I find in giving gifts, this is a shoo-in. In fact, a few years ago I decided to count all the projects I have around the house that could be built with existing materials. I asked myself how long I could stay home without having to buy anything—anything at all—to add to what I had on hand, and it turned out to be seven years. *Seven years*? That is pack-ratting to the max.

All my life I've bought the makings for hobbies, crafts, baskets, birdhouses, jewelry, models, books—like most women buy salad greens. And this doesn't count the number of things I'd like to make from apple crates, pine cones, Popsicle sticks, wine corks, watercolors, mosaics, and old furniture.

A friend was unwrapping a gift I had given her several years ago as she said over and over, "I hope this is handmade. Is it handmade?" Knowing I hadn't made it, and fearing she would be disappointed, I finally asked, "What if it isn't handmade, Ruth? What'll happen then? Will you keep it anyway?"

She looked me straight in the face and said in all seriousness, "I'll give you another chance." I thought that was hilarious, but it stuck with me. It made me wish I had made the gift, and it also made me realize how much people love handmade gifts. Because, when you give them that gift, you're not only giving them the object, you're giving them something money can't buy—your time and creativity.

I was at a friend's home for dinner and admired his dining table. Beautiful wood, perfectly planed, and polished to a high shine. I could tell he was proud of it. I said, "Wow, Dave, where'd you get this? It's wonderful. I've never seen anything quite like it." It sort of resembled a harvest table. A little narrower than most, but big enough to accommodate folks for a robust Thanksgiving dinner.

Proudly, while rubbing the top of the table with his hand, he said, "I made this out of seven old church pews, Luci. Found them and thought they were too beautiful to sit around just collecting dust. I had to cut and measure carefully to be sure I did it right, but when I finished, I thought it turned out pretty well. Glad you like it."

"I love it, Dave. You did a great job. Is Cathy pleased?" That's his wife.

"Oh yeah. I made it for her."

I knew just how Dave felt. The joy of taking the time, doing things carefully, building something with our hands to give to someone else—even if it's nothing more than a greeting card or a delicious meal—evokes a thrill in us that's hard to describe. But to do this with everything I give away? Well, that's the mother of all maybes.

STAR IN THE *DIE HARD* MOVIES

Yeah, it's the truth. Sorry if you're offended. (Well, not really . . .) I love those films and own the whole set of videos. I also own all the *Lethal Weapon* movies. More than once I've spent an evening watching one and enjoyed it all over again. I might could watch one tonight, now that I think about it. But to star in one would be the ultimate fun. A true adventure.

I have friends who won't go to anything but "Boy Meets Girl" movies. They are so boringly predictable (not the friends, the movies). Boy meets girl. Girl wears cute clothes. Boy and girl fall in love. Boy and girl get married. Boy and girl have baby. I'd much rather see something that makes me think or keeps me on the edge of my seat. I tried to talk one of these friends into seeing *Silence of the Lambs*. She was reluctant because she was a "boy meets girl" movie freak. But she finally agreed to go, and we had fun.

I've got just enough acting lessons under my belt and am hammy enough to think starring in a good ol' action/adventure *Die Hard* movie would be the thrill of a lifetime. And who's to say I can't or I won't? Nobody. So I added it here because I'm just daring enough to dream about it. Besides, I think Bruce Willis is pretty cute.

Hey! Anything's possible. Life reeks with possibilities. (I love the word *reek*. It's very direct—that word means business.) And I'd love it if everybody desired to reek with adventure. Go out there and grab it by the throat and mean business!

I read an article about a woman who, at the age of eighty-seven, finished college and got her degree. Her name was Anne Martindell. She started classes at Smith College in 1932 as a freshman, but after a year her father, a federal judge, forced her to leave because he was afraid she'd be too educated to find a husband. Can you beat that?

In the interim, she served as U.S. ambassador to New Zealand, a New Jersey state senator, and head of the U.S. Office of Foreign Disaster Assistance. She married and divorced twice, had four children, nine grandchildren, and two great-grandchildren. In 1996, feeling a void in her life, she decided to take the advice of a loved one and enroll in Smith's educational program designed for older women who wanted to return to class. After that auspicious beginning in 1932, she earned her diploma in 2002. She also received an honorary doctorate at the same time.

The program's founding director told the reporter that when Mrs. Martindell first came back to campus she walked with a cane, but within weeks it disappeared, and in no time she was revitalized. "There was a spring in her step and a gleam in her eye," the director said.

What better describes adventure? It's letting your personal vision and dreams take you to new heights and new beginnings. Lauren Bacall once said, "Imagination is the highest kite one can fly"—so true.

Let's take hold of the string, fly away to where it takes us, and who knows? We might could even wind up on the moon.

As we grow older, the more
frequently we look back in remembrance.

_____

_____

_____

_____

_____

_____

_____

_____

_____

_____

_____

_____

_____

_____

_____

_____

_____

_____

_____

_____

Imagination is the highest kite one can fly.

—*Lauren Bacall*

_____

_____

_____

_____

_____

_____

_____

_____

_____

_____

_____

_____

_____

_____

_____

_____

_____

_____

_____

_____

_____

_____

_____

The ability to think is a wonderful gift. We take it for granted, yet what would it be like if we couldn't remember, evaluate, determine, make plans, decide right from wrong, or change our minds?

_____

_____

_____

_____

_____

_____

_____

_____

_____

_____

_____

_____

_____

_____

_____

_____

_____

What are the things in life
you cannot imagine living without?

_____

_____

_____

_____

_____

_____

_____

_____

_____

_____

_____

_____

_____

_____

_____

_____

_____

_____

_____

_____

This is my idea of a perfect day: Get up at 7 a.m., enjoy a cup of Starbucks with breakfast on the patio, work in my garden for an hour deadheading plants and gathering a bouquet of fresh flowers for the dining table. Talk on the phone with a few friends, work at my computer, journal a bit, leisurely read the paper, and have a wonderful lunch of baked chicken, broccoli, tossed salad, and dessert while watching *Law and Order*. Spend the afternoon painting or making something fun, e-mailing friends or writing a letter. Read, listen to music, and wind down the day with the ABC news. Take a bicycle ride through the neighborhood about dusk. Light dinner, then popcorn while watching an old movie or reading a great book. A warm bubble bath and to bed between clean, white sheets about 11 p.m. This is heaven on earth.

How often do I get it? Maybe once a year if I'm lucky!

That kind of a day might bore you to death, but being at home with little or nothing to do is a luxury for me. As much as I travel, when I'm home, I'm ecstatic for the first couple of days. It would take a tornado to get me out of the house. I love cooking, projects, putzing, gardening, and simply being there. I could spend weeks indoors without ever getting cabin fever. Home is my haven, my place of refuge, and my joy. I even wait until I'm down to bare cupboards before grocery shopping. It just isn't worth it for Mother Hubbard to leave home. And when I do shop, I try to buy everything I can imagine, so I don't have to go again for another six weeks. Errands get in the way of all the things I love doing at home. I've often said if I got fired from Women of Faith, I'd stay home for a solid year just to make up for lost time.

Before I moved to the home I'm living in now (in Texas), I lived in a 1,547 square foot condo . . . and loved it. One would've thought I'd scream after two hours in such small quarters, but that's not the case. In fact—the opposite was true. I couldn't seem to get enough solitude in that cozy spot.

My favorite spot in the house was my walk-in closet (only forty-two square feet). I turned it into an itsy-bitsy art studio. Took out the bars for hanging clothes, added corbels to hold up the shelves, painted the whole thing a wonderful Matisse yellow, changed sliding wooden doors into bifold louvered doors, and converted the whole thing into a wonderful workplace.

All my how-to books were on the shelf in there—how to paint, draw, weave, macramé, build kites, clocks, paper animals, and toys. There was a drafting table and chair, a cabinet with cute, narrow drawers—all of which I built. (Don't ever try to build a drafting chair yourself. The directions are written by an alien from another planet in a language we know not of and left unfinished because he shot himself mid-project out of confusion and desperation.) It took me three full days to figure the thing out, and every time I sat in it I wasn't sure it was made right. I always had a feeling it would fold up on me one day and become a tree.

From the ceiling I hung two mobiles. A small toy bear rode along a string on a unicycle from one wall to the other, balancing weights in both hands. There were stickers, watercolors, china paints, stamps, buckets of brushes and pencils, Lego toys, rulers, a portable light table, framed drawings, photos and quotations, posters, ball caps, stuffed toys, a world globe, handwoven rug, tiny electric fan, telephone, portable CD player with two

speakers, and a blow-up plastic model of *The Scream* by Edvard Munch. When I wanted to completely forget the world and my concerns, this is where I'd go. Shut the door behind me and stay for hours. Ah, bliss! I've often said *it doesn't take a lot to make me happy—just the right thing.* That studio was the right thing.

One of the reasons I love home is because I was sixty-one before I owned one. I've always lived in fun places I've fixed up from beginning to end, but it wasn't until the early 1990s that I even

...in my wonderful little 42☐' Studio. I LOVE IT ☺!

thought of buying my own place. Spent my money on travel. Because I didn't have enough for both, I chose to see the world first. Now, late in life, I own a home that's filled with memorabilia collected from my trips around the world. No regrets.

The place where I live will never grow old or boring or commonplace, because it has my whole life in it, so to speak—artwork, books, music, photographs, furnishings. Everything speaks of the life I dreamed about when I was growing up. It's chock-full of memories. Having a little place that reflects my history, character, travels, tastes, and preferences is more important to me than filling it with the most expensive furnishings chosen by a decorator. When the world is pulling at me to do more, be more, acquire more, my home says to me, "Enough already. Everything I need is here." That corny, little hackneyed phrase "There's no place like home" has my name written all over it.

I've always valued having a space of my own. As far back as I can remember, I had my own room, fixed it up the way I wanted, arranged my cubicle at the office to suit me, designated a little spot as mine when I was in double-occupancy hotel rooms. Even on an airplane, I like to surround myself with my own things. That's why I don't prefer the bulkhead—I can't put things under my feet!

This sense of place gives me a feeling of well-being—ill-founded as it may be. Leo Buscaglia writes in *Bus Nine to Paradise*, "We all need our separate worlds, apart from others, where we can quietly retire for regrouping, for getting back in touch with ourselves. We need this personal solitary place as a pleasant alternative to our more public lives. We must treasure this part of our existence as much as we do the more social part. Then, when loneliness comes, we will have that special place to fall back upon."[18] So, when I had the option to buy a house, I was all for it. Ready and excited and determined to make it comfortable, accessible to my loved ones, and filled with the treasures I've spent a lifetime collecting. Being a person who loves to contemplate and reflect, my home gives me a quiet place to do that. I have a little tile someone gave me that reads, "Anything for a quiet life."

There is a wonderful little verse tucked away in Proverbs 21. It says, "An upright man gives thought to his ways" (v. 29). Thinking about the ways I have come through life—mental pursuits, adventures, straights and narrows—I know now there are things I would never want to miss. They make up my core and they are as vital as the blood in my veins. You've seen them throughout this book, but I want to define them specifically here because they're the indexes out of which I make life choices. I cannot imagine my life without . . .

CHASING AFTER BEAUTY

My mother first introduced me to beauty. She insisted if I was setting the table that I use the "good dishes" and that they all match. She loved fresh flowers and often picked bouquets for the dining table or coffee table when I was a child. I've seen her cry over beautiful poetry, music, or art. And as far back as I can remember, she encouraged all three of her children to love and take time for beauty. She used to say to me, "You don't have to necessarily understand it to feel deeply about it. You may never understand what moves you, but if it does, it'll be with you forever." Oh, the times I have taken something with me forever that I didn't understand. I wanted to understand because I have a penchant for "knowing," but I realized something had happened inside me that, albeit inexplicable, had changed me forever.

I was reading about Africa and pulled a book off my shelf called *Tapestries from Egypt*. I began glancing through it and marveled at the beautiful pictures—all in color. As I was getting ready to put the book away, the flyleaf fell open. In the front I had inscribed, "To my mother . . . the first person who gave me a love for beauty! Merry Christmas. 1969."

I wouldn't trade anything for the encouragement from Mother at such a young age. The author Simone Weil wrote in *Gateway to God*:

> To pay no attention to the world's beauty is, perhaps, so great a crime of ingratitude that it deserves the punishment of affliction. To be sure, it does not always get it; but then the alternative punishment is a mediocre life, and in what way is a mediocre life preferable to affliction?[19]

Pursuing beauty is one of the hallmarks of my life. I want to go to my grave running after it wherever I can find it. I'll always be looking for it in every nook and cranny.

SEEING THE WORLD

In my years of foreign travel, I have managed to visit every continent, and I have loved every trip. In addition to a wonderful cruise starting in New Zealand and ending up at the Sydney Opera House in Australia, I've been to Israel, Ethiopia, Rwanda, and a trip on the Nile River in Egypt. Even as I write this, I have reservations to go on a Reformation Tour with a group from Insight for Living, led by my brother, Chuck. We'll go to the Czech Republic, Switzerland, and Germany—and see the Passion Play in Oberammergau.

Plans are also in the offing for a trip to the Orient. They may never materialize, but they're on the table for consideration. Every year I pore over travel guides and study different places in the world on maps and the Internet. *Where can I go next?* is a common question I ask myself. I don't think I'll ever get my fill of trotting around the globe.

GOING THE EXTRA MILE

The greatest adventures of my life have come because I said yes to the unknown.

When I was asked to take a management position at Mobil, I remember being scared to death. I didn't think I could do the job. I had never held a position where so many major decisions would rest on my shoulders. An enormous budget would be under my stewardship, and I would be responsible for the performance of personnel at my direction. It was way out of my comfort zone. But something in me told me I could do it. I had the feeling the doing of it would come from a force outside myself. I was going to simply be the instrument to get the job done. So I took the position. And I did it. And I'm so glad.

When I first started traveling, I had no extra money. Everything I made went toward basic living expenses. But I so wanted to go that I agreed to do it with a friend, and we worked on the details together, split-ting the financial load. That's when I saved twenty-five dollars a month for five years. There wasn't a month it was easy, because I had to sacrifice in some other area to do it. But when the time came to go, not only did I have enough to make the trip, but also enough to financially help the sister of my friend who had wanted to join us but couldn't afford it. The three of us made that first trip in 1966, and I'm so glad. It set in motion trips I have made on a tight budget all my life. Where there's a will, there's a way. I'm living proof!

More than thirty years after my first trip to Europe, one of the most exciting things I did was cruise around the coast of South America with three of my closest friends. It was our Christmas vacation. I took on board about a hundred wooden children's blocks and, from them, built a tiny Christmas tree for our stateroom. I covered the blocks with tiny ornaments, glitter, decorations, stars, and baubles. The gifts we took along were all small, wrapped in green, blue, red, or gold paper with beautiful ribbon, and everything was placed on top of the television set. I made the tree the first day I was on the cruise (December 14), and we ogled it for fifteen days. Other passengers came to see it. Our cabin attendant admired it and took her own photographs.

On Christmas Day, after attending a church service on the ship, we had a big Christmas dinner; then the four of us spent the rest of the day enjoy-ing one another. We first had our own little service in our room . . . at the foot of the tiny tree. We prayed together, thanking God for our years of friendship, that wonderful trip, the goodness of the Lord, and the countless blessings that had come to us from the extension of his gracious hand. Then we opened gifts. Lots of laughter. And tears. And picture taking. And yelling over what was received. No one can take away that memory from us.

This is what going the extra mile is all about. I gave serious thought to not carting all those little wooden blocks on the trip. They were heavy and took up precious space. And not only the blocks, but a box of tiny decora-tions, glue gun, tissue paper, wrapping paper, and ribbon. But in the end it was so worth it. I dismantled the tree when it was all over, put it away, packed it in my suitcase, and three years later, built it all again for the coffee table in my living room. South America revisited!

The point I'm making is that if we bite off a bit more than we think we can chew, the Lord brings something into play that wasn't there until we took the bite. It was the philosophy of Henry David Thoreau: "If one advances confidently in the direction of his dreams, and endeavors to live the life which he has imagined, he will meet with a success unexpected in common hours." The operative word in his comment is "meet." It is in that meeting of our saying yes and the work of the Holy Spirit that the thing gets accomplished. Human spirit meets up with the Holy Spirit and—*bam!*— the adventure begins.

God never calls that he doesn't enable. I believe in striking out and watching him work out the details. Once we start something, a momentum begins that propels us toward completion. But it takes really wanting to do it to get started. There's no drive-through breakthrough in life. Nothing of value can be had for nothing.

RECORDING MY SURROUNDINGS

"Please take notes." This is a huge value to me. I've recorded information on the palm of my hand, on the back of envelopes, on the sides of cans or buckets. I've written something while driving or as a passenger. Once, on the back of a donkey in Greece, I wanted to remember directions on how to get back, so I drew a map on my shorts . . . while bumping along on the donkey.

I have never regretted what I wrote down but have often regretted what I didn't. Trying to remember is harder as the years go by, so it is very important to me that I keep a chronicle of my life. As Hannah Hinchman, the graphic artist and journalist, says, "One of the dangers of life without a journal is that we would have to entrust the events of our lives to memory alone." The older I get I see how that would never work for me. My journals are for me, not necessarily anybody else. Just so I can read them, remember when I wrote that, and be glad I took notes. Everybody needs a sanctuary for her memories, and my journal is mine. If you ever want to keep a journal yourself, just take your life as it is at this moment, and start writing about it.

STAYING IN TOUCH

I am a very loyal person. The people I love may be a small circle, but I always want to let them know how I much I care about them. This is vitally important to me. If I'm with them, I'll tell them how I feel, and if we're apart, I want to call or write or e-mail my feelings. I learned this from my dad, and it's ingrained in my personality. It's actually part of my temperament. No matter how old I get, staying in touch will always be part of my daily life. If I'm traveling abroad, I especially want to stay in touch. And when I don't have access to e-mail in some foreign country, it drives me crazy. I don't remember a single time of traveling where I didn't phone home at least once to speak with those who mean so much to me.

My whole family is like that—what's left of us. Each of my brothers is a wonderful correspondent. They're good at staying in touch by letters, e-mails, thank-you notes, packages, gifts, and phone calls. We learned this early on from our parents. As a little girl, I don't ever remember returning home after visiting Momo and Granddaddy when Mother didn't say, "Be sure to write them a thank-you note." And, she'd often add, "Draw a little picture on the note. They'll love that."

I've got mountains of saved correspondence from my siblings, friends, and business associates. A lot of it is in my bulging journals, tucked away to be read over and over. I even have an old note written to my mother from her mother. It reads, "Going next door to borrow an egg." That note is staying in touch to the nth degree!

CELEBRATING THE FINISH LINE

One of my favorite activities in life is celebrating. Anything. I don't really need a reason. I wrote a book on that whole idea: *You Bring the Confetti, God Brings the Joy*. I don't understand why many people don't celebrate completions. There are millions of opportunities to celebrate. Here's a simple example.

I have been on as many as fifty different diets in my lifetime, and one of the most exciting was clearly designed for people like me. Very regimented, detailed, involved, and full of celebrations along the way. I dieted on this program in 1979, and it was totally successful. It was called the No Choice Diet and was exactly as the title implied. You had to obey it to the letter or little men in white coats would take you away to a fat farm.

In a nutshell, here was the regimen: It lasted thirty-three days and promised the loss of ten pounds. Each day had a given diet and fitness program to follow exactly—morning, daytime, and evening. Begin on Monday. Don't skip ahead in the book. Read each page as you come to it, and once that page is finished, tear it out and throw it away. There were pictures and drawings of exercises to follow, which only added to my joy.

But here is what put me over the top with exuberance—a little paragraph on page 10 entitled "Reward Yourself." This paragraph encouraged the participant to celebrate progress. At the loss of three pounds, you gave yourself a present. At five pounds, another present. At eight pounds, another one. On and on it went. When the total ten pounds were lost, you were to reward yourself with "something that you can wear or keep prominently displayed, which symbolizes your achievement. It could be a gold chain, a picture you love, or an interesting piece of sculpture." I loved this diet!

But get this—I made it even more fun. I kept lists each week of the groceries I bought and made a chart that I hung on my refrigerator on which I recorded progress week after week. I was driven and, needless to say, lost weight and had a great time doing it. What kept me going was not only the recording of data but also the celebrations along the way.

The only thing I did not obey was that I didn't tear out and throw away the pages (so I'm writing the rest of this from the fat farm). I just couldn't bring myself to do that, pack rat that I am. If you want to see all this stuff—the book, charts, grocery lists—give me a call, and I can show it to you. This diet incorporated everything that turns my crank: figuring it out, regimenting myself, keeping notes on the progress, celebrating along the way, and accomplishing a self-imposed task. It was a wonderful adventure.

I firmly believe the Lord has led me every step of the way into a life of adventures worth remembering and celebrating. Through the years he's opened door after door of possibility. Some of those doors I've walked through, others I haven't. Even as a youngster, though, I was a dreamer. But the insatiability of youth was burdensome, never acknowledging human limitations. It always sought much but was capable of little. Now, at seventy-seven, so many of my dreams have come true. I've followed the road map, and although I can't see very far ahead, I feel certain I'm going in the right direction.

There is no doubt I've missed many joys and advantages from not having a spouse and family. Nevertheless, I would still choose the life I've known. If the Lord took me today, I wouldn't look back regretting I never married. But I might look back regretting I didn't climb Mount Everest or spend a week in a submarine or become a translator for the Federal Bureau of Investigation.

The most important thing for each of us is to embrace and celebrate life for what it is. Being alive is a gift, and we will never exhaust all the adventures or possibilities that are ours because Jesus Christ has provided an inexhaustible legacy for us, established before the foundation of the world. Every day he opens new doors for us to walk through. He gives us a new way of looking at old problems. He challenges us to take him at his word as we consider how to resolve different dilemmas. He assures us of his constant presence. And here's the best adventure of all—he lives in us! We can go anywhere and do anything, because the one who leads us never fails. As the old hymn says:

> *The King of love my Shepherd is, whose goodness faileth never;*
> *I nothing lack if I am His and He is mine forever. . . .*

> *In death's dark vale I fear no ill with Thee, dear Lord, beside me;*
> *Thy rod and staff my comfort still, Thy cross before to guide me. . . .*

> *And so through all the length of days Thy goodness faileth never;*
> *Good Shepherd, may I sing Thy praise within Thy house forever.*[20]

Capturing the moment is found in the willingness to go the extra mile. Describe a time you lived out of this truth.

_____

_____

_____

_____

_____

_____

_____

_____

_____

_____

_____

_____

_____

_____

_____

_____

_____

_____

Postcards are the greatest way in the world to capture the moment.
They're colorful, easy to acquire, quick to write, and inexpensive.
Write a postcard to yourself about a favorite moment.

Every person who dared to live the life she dreamed started by learning the explosive force of God's lessons. Her soul was liberated from its prison, and life began to have genuine meaning.

_____

_____

_____

_____

_____

_____

_____

_____

_____

_____

_____

_____

_____

_____

_____

_____

_____

_____

CANON AE 1
w/24mm 1:28 Lens
(wide angle)

CAPTURING THE DIFFERENCE

PART 6

In 2009 I visited Rwanda. I'd known of the genocide there in 1994 but was not prepared to hear firsthand about the horror that had actually erupted. However, through the devastation, there were those who found hope and God's provision in what can only be described as a miracle. Chantal Kagaba is one of those miracles.

Chantal was twenty-one years old in 1994, pregnant, and living in Rwanda's capital city, Kigali, with her husband, Alex, and their four-year-old daughter, Vanessa. The genocide broke out on April 6 between two neighboring tribes: the Hutus and Tutsis. These two tribes had lived side by side as friends, families, and coworkers, but suddenly, and for seemingly no reason, civil war erupted between them. What ensued was one hundred days of slaughter, and Chantal was caught in the storm.

She was at the home of her sister when the radio announced that nobody could move about the country. The president of Rwanda had been killed. Alex was stuck in a hotel, and Vanessa was home with the babysitter. Alex called Chantal, saying, "Don't worry; I'll get out and come to you and Vanessa." The next morning Alex was killed. His last words to Chantal had been, "I love you."

When she finally got to Vanessa, Chantal found her hiding under a table crying. She grabbed her and ran.

For weeks they ran, hiding in ditches, hungry, crawling over dead bodies, asking for help, staying in the bush—wondering all the while if they would survive. On June 12, concealed in a pile of banana leaves, Chantal gave birth to "little Alex." Vanessa ran for help and came back with a woman who happened to be a nurse. She helped Chantal, and then she, too, fled.

In time the genocide ended, but in the hearts of people like Chantal who had endured it, the pain was not erased. However, in spite of her horror, she learned to forgive.

During court hearings later, a man named Felix confessed that he had killed Chantal's parents. Felix explained that after he and others had beaten Chantal's mother, she said to them, "I know you are going to kill me, but do you mind if I pray for you?" After her prayer, she faced her executioners and said, "Now I'm ready to join my Jesus. If you ever meet one of my children, tell them I've prayed for you and have forgiven you." Then Felix shot her.

In time, Chantal visited Felix in prison. He was afraid to see her because he knew she hated him. But she said, "Don't worry Felix. I know you killed my mom, even though she was innocent. But I've done a worse thing to you. In my heart, I've killed you and all your family. But now, the purpose of my visit is to ask for forgiveness." Through his tears, Felix forgave her.

Chantal's story is far beyond anything I could ever imagine personally. But what she learned is what we must all learn when we are wronged, when life disappoints us, or when we feel hopeless: "It's what we trust in but don't yet see that keeps us going" (2 Corinthians 5:7). By God's grace, we learn, just as Chantal did, to do life differently. We trust. We don't seek revenge. We give out of the grace of God that has been given to us. It's not something we do naturally. Doing life differently can only be done supernaturally, by the power of the love of God working within us, enabling us to live as he did, regardless of the circumstances.

Vergia Fears was a young girl I met when I was first employed by Mobil Oil Corporation back in the 1950s. She worked in the mail room, and I enjoyed her so much. We called her Verge. She was tall, thin, black, beautiful, and as sharp as a tack. Everything that came out of her mouth was either funny or profound. I loved it when mail needed to be delivered to my office because she'd stand at my drafting table and chat.

One day we started talking about books—what kind we liked, what we were reading, different authors, whether we preferred fiction or nonfiction. Verge stopped for a few seconds then said, "You know, Lucille . . . one day I'm gonna write a book."

"Really? Do you have a title in mind?"

"Oh yeah. I'm gonna call it *Noah Steps Out*."

"*Noah Steps Out*? Gosh, that's great, Verge. I love that title. How did you come up with it?"

She looked straight into my eyes and said in all seriousness, "I've thought about it for years. Can you imagine how Noah felt when he opened the door on that boat and saw a world he'd never seen before? After the storm everything was different. He musta been wonderin' what things were gonna look like. And then, there it was—stuff he never dreamed of right in front of his eyes. He liked it . . . so he stepped out."

In all these years, I've never forgotten that conversation with my friend nor the concept of her book idea. I don't know where Verge is now, but her words will be in my head forever. When she turned to leave the room, she looked back over her shoulder, with a twinkle in her eye. "I'll have to change my last name though. Authors do that all the time, I guess. I'll be called Vergia Fearnot."

"Good idea, Verge. Fearnot's a great name. Besides, it'd be hard for a person named Fears to sell a book about a guy who stepped out on faith."

"That's what I was thinkin'," she said, then smiled and walked away.

When I finished writing *I Married Adventure*, it felt like my whole story was completed. *It's a wrap*, I thought. It contained my philosophy of life and the many ways God continually reinforced that philosophy as he led me all those years. And I have to say, I feel exactly the same now as I did when that book was published in 2003—I hold to the same beliefs, enjoy the same friends, am moved by the same music, drama, and paintings, appreciate the same adventures. But, what I *hadn't* imagined back then that I know now is that God was constantly expanding my heart. He wanted me to open the door, step out, and enjoy what I hadn't seen before. He began showing me new ways to trust him.

I could have named this last part of the book "Luci Steps Out," because that's exactly what happened after I wrote the first fifteen chapters. As content as I was then, God began creating a new heart in me— one that was ready for different challenges and unfamiliar ways of doing things.

It's strange, because with the gift of years, I always thought I'd be slowing down somewhat due to aging. But instead, the momentum of my life has seemingly picked up, and the rewards of God's grace have been almost mind-boggling at times. He is giving me more and more capacity to have an even richer life in my seventies. Who knew that would happen? I stepped into the unknown by faith, and he blessed and honored that step in a million ways. When I take time to look carefully at my life, I often think of this scripture from 1 Corinthians 2:9:

> No one's ever seen or heard anything like this,
> Never so much as imagined anything quite like it—
> What God has arranged for those who love him. (MSG)

And here's the best part—God will do the same for anyone. He'll do it for you.

When I was about thirteen years old, I was too young to know exactly what I wanted, but for the most part, I can tell you what I didn't want. I didn't want routine. I loved my parents, but there was something in me that wanted more than their "norm." I couldn't see myself settling down in a small Texas town when I finished high school. I wanted to go to college. I wanted to travel around the world. I wanted to read, go to art museums, study music, sing in the opera, learn other languages. I wanted a big, huge, wonderful life. Both my brothers made decisions at a very early age to marry and go into the ministry. I didn't want to do that, for sure. I wanted to be different, do different things, go different places, live differently. Whatever that meant, it didn't mean settling down. I'm sure my parents looked at me at times, shaking their heads, thinking, *Oh honey.* But somewhere inside I knew what I wanted, and looking back on it, I believe it was a dream God planted inside my heart, maybe from the womb. That's the dream I wanted to pursue. It was enormous, textured, and full of life.

But what I didn't realize is that my dream was small compared to the one God had for me. His avenues of discovery were so much greater than I could have imagined. I took a baby step, trusting God to open doors for me, only to discover that my tiny imagination was the tip of the iceberg compared to what he had planned.

God's dream for my life didn't look like the one my parents had for me, nor did it look like the one I had for myself. His was fuller, richer, sweeter, and more than anyone could visualize. Not my parents, not my friends, and certainly not I. His dream continues to unfold, while I stand around being amazed! And when I thought it couldn't get any better than this, it did, and it does! Here's what's wonderful—the unfolding of his dream is not because of me and what I do; it's totally because of him and what he does. It's because of who he is.

I never married nor had children. However, I see how God's plan for me included children, but not in the traditional way. In 1999, when Women of Faith began a partnership with World Vision, I was invited to go to Guatemala with them to see their relief work and learn more about their global outreach. I went solely for the adventure of seeing the country—but God had all that and more in mind for me. In fact, I told my friends with whom I was traveling that I knew World Vision probably wanted me to sponsor a child in Guatemala, but I wasn't going to do it. "I hope they know I'm not into that," I said. "I don't want the responsibility of sponsoring a child or getting attached to one."

Well! That was just the beginning of God's plan. Not only did I meet and fall in love with little five-year-old Blanca Estella Boch while there, but I began sponsoring her and have been doing so every month for the past ten years. Nobody coerced me into it, nor even asked me. I just found my heart couldn't resist. A couple weeks ago I got a picture from her, a letter, and her latest drawing. She writes me frequently, thanking me for loving her and helping her. It melts my heart.

And Blanca was the first of my "family abroad." Now I sponsor two other girls—Harmonie from the Congo and Yessica from the Dominican Republic, as well as Patrick, a little boy from Kenya. I even have the privilege of sponsoring an entire family in Ghana. Abena Gyambea is the matriarch with five children. She also cares for her granddaughter and aunt. (You'll remember reading about my time in Ghana, in chapter 6.) Obviously, God wanted me to have children.

I never planned on all that. But that's the whole point—the minute I opened the door and stepped out, God made it happen. Being involved in the work of World Vision has become one of the greatest joys of my life. Traveling with that organization has taken me to Guatemala, India, South Africa, Kenya, Ghana, Rwanda, and Ethiopia. I also have a feeling that my twelve sponsored individuals, whom I love and care for, are a drop in the bucket compared to the additional children I'll be sponsoring in the years ahead.

There's no way we can know in advance what God is going to do with our lives. Our dreams are small compared to his. He takes our hearts and fashions them into something that perfectly matches his design for us. He knew I wanted to visit every continent, so he let me do it. But, he added to it his desire for me to be open to the needs I saw. Once I recognized that and learned how I could help, even more doors opened. It's become a way of life now. When I stopped trying to make it all happen, it happened anyway because of him. Look at Proverbs 3:5–6:

Trust God from the bottom of your heart;
   don't try to figure out everything on your own.
Listen for God's voice in everything you do, everywhere you go;
   he's the one who will keep you on track. (MSG)

God let me go everywhere I wanted to, see the countries I was curious about, but the end result is his gift of my being able to help these wonderful children. I wanted to do my life differently, and he knew that. So right smack in the middle of it, he had me doing *his* will too. It's amazing to me. We rarely stop to think about it, but when we do, we're baffled. Thrilled. Over the moon. We can't figure it out. God uses us as conduits of his love and provision. What a way to live.

Another big surprise God had for me was to design and build my own home.

It was New Year's Eve of 2003 when Marilyn and I were talking about whether I might move to Dallas. At the time, I was living in a small condo I had purchased nine years before in Palm Desert, California. Until 1994 I rented apartments, but I bought a little condo that year because I found that if I moved to the desert, it was less expensive than leasing the place where I was living in Orange County.

However, in time, Palm Desert was too out of the way for all the traveling I was doing with Women of Faith. The WOF offices are near Dallas, and week after week as I flew through Dallas, I watched staff members get off planes at their destination while I had another three hours to go. "If you lived here, you'd be home now," they'd often say. In fact, during the busy traveling season, I finally wound up staying in the home of friends who lived in the Dallas area for months on end. In 2003 I was their guest for six months. (They have to be the most gracious hostesses in the nation to put up with me all that time. But they couldn't have been sweeter with my being their constant houseguest.) Finally, just to make it easier on me, they encouraged me to consider moving to Dallas. Because homes in their area were more affordable than in California, I was very tempted. Being close to

SEEING THE LIFE I NEVER IMAGINED

friends, family, my brother's church, and more than half the WOF cities to which we traveled had a lot of appeal.

After having lived in Southern California for thirty years, I knew moving to another state would be complicated and very expensive. Nevertheless, I decided to investigate the possibility. All my mental wheels went into motion. I first met with a financial adviser to get his perspective on the cost. Then I talked with a real estate agent who actually lived a few houses down my street in the desert. I consulted with a builder in Texas to check out the expense of designing and building a home to my liking. Finally, being convinced this was the right thing to do, I hired a moving company to pack up my stuff in California, take it to Texas, and put it in storage until the house was finished. My closest friends and family joined me in asking the Lord's guidance throughout the entire undertaking. And after much prayer and weighing pros and cons with these dear people, I decided to move to Frisco, Texas, a lovely community just north of Dallas. On January 27, 2004, I signed the "Contract for Sale and Purchase" to build the home of my choosing. Everything in the whole process was God's grace. When there were tests and trials during those seven months of building, I hung on to Hebrews 10:35–36:

Don't throw it all away now. . . . you need to stick it out, staying with God's plan so you'll be there for the promised completion. (MSG)

And if I got discouraged when everything seemed overwhelming, I'd reread the notes I'd written in my journal as I went along. Here's an entry from January 28, just as my condo went on the market to sell:

You know, Journal, it's a strange thing, but I feel I'm a pawn on a chess board in this whole thing. It's way out of my realm. God is doing it. He's selling this condo, not me! I couldn't change the course of things if I tried. It's out of my hands. There's a little propeller on my heart, moving things along toward a certain destination. Even when I might want to say "no" or "not so fast" or "maybe," it's as though God says what HE wants to and his words come out of my mouth. Amazingly, I'm not afraid or worried as I go down this winding path. Let him figure it out. It's beyond my understanding. It's the flow of sovereignty . . . ever moving forward.

Even as I read that again today after five years, I can tell you I still feel inside my heart what I felt then. Maybe you've been through seasons like that. You know you're doing the right thing, and you can't stop it, because there's something about it that's totally out of your control. It's like my friend Verge told me, "You step out . . . and fear not." There's no way to explain it.

Once I made the decision to go through with it, here's what happened: My condo sold within a week of going on the market for over twice what I paid for it. I got back the largest income tax refund I've ever received in my life. I built the house in Texas that I wanted and dedicated it to the Lord on April 7, 2004. Written in the cement foundation is the line:

This house is dedicated to God. 04/07/04. L. Swindoll

I took possession of the house on August 11 and moved in on Labor Day, 2004. It's everything I ever dreamed and more. It has the library I always wanted and the wall space to hang paintings and artwork I've collected all my life (including original paintings by my mother and aunt). It has a gorgeous landscaped yard and patio so I can sit outside on spring days. There's a small studio where I can work, paint, build things, and create greeting cards and drawings. And when I'm through working or tired, I simply close the door and walk straight into my library . . . or kitchen. Mostly, my house is a gathering place for my loved ones. They come, go, have a cup of coffee, dinner, spend the night, or spend a week. Or they just drop by. I'm more delighted by that than I can even express in words.

I've had dinner parties here in my library-dining area, photo shoots for Women of Faith, business meetings for the company, Christmas and birthday celebrations, and gatherings of all sorts. And to round out God's grace—the house is paid for!

Over time, many of my closest friends have moved into the area. I'm surrounded by people I love and around whom my life revolves. My brother, Chuck Swindoll, and his family live half a mile away, and the church he pastors is about two miles from me. I hear him preach every Sunday and am encircled by family members right and left. And since I believe Chuck's the best Bible teacher on the planet—I'm lovin' it. Neither of us could have imagined that at this time in our lives we'd live a hop, skip, and a jump from one another. Even my parents couldn't have dreamed this up.

Both my brothers have spent their lifetimes in ministry. Not I. My desire was to have a career, and that's where God led me for the first forty years of my adult life. How could I have known that when I retired, God had another life in store for me? One I never could have imagined. (Although I'm somewhat suspicious it's the answer to my mother's prayers!) When I was invited to join Women of Faith and I opened that door, all my thinking about not wanting a ministry changed. And it changed me! And, not only me . . . but by the end of 2008, over 267,000 women from all over the nation were changed. They had put their faith in Christ, and he came to live in them and give them hope, joy, and victory in their circumstances. Millions have attended our events since 1996, and amazingly, our team feels a special bond with them all—even though there are so many.

Our perspective changes when we trust the Lord to be the Guardian and Guide of our lives. Everything is different—goals, plans, finances, emotions, coping patterns, sickness, health, desires. When we have Christ, we do life differently. It all takes on new meaning. God makes his presence known over and over in every way under the sun, and the fun and joy of living comes back into our environment. He works in our behalf and teaches us his principles as we go along. All we have to do is open the door. Step out. Trust him. And see what we never imagined. Don't be afraid. Never, ever be afraid.

We are each a combination of many factors woven together
out of the joys and sorrows of life. We're the product of our choices.
We're the result of what was done for us or to us by our parents.
What were the ingredients that made you who you are?

_____

_____

_____

_____

_____

_____

_____

_____

_____

_____

_____

_____

_____

_____

_____

_____

_____

_____

God creates each of us uniquely by his design and for his purpose.
He readies the path that takes us toward his desired end.

_____

_____

_____

_____

_____

_____

_____

_____

_____

_____

_____

_____

_____

_____

_____

_____

_____

_____

*The real voyage of discovery consists not in seeking
new landscapes, but in having new eyes.*

—Marcel Proust

_____

_____

_____

_____

_____

_____

_____

_____

_____

_____

_____

_____

_____

_____

_____

_____

_____

_____

When we start trusting God outside our comfort zone,
anything can happen, anywhere. Describe a time you trusted
God outside your comfort zone and what happened.

_____

_____

_____

_____

_____

_____

_____

_____

_____

_____

_____

_____

_____

_____

_____

_____

_____

CHAPTER 17: *Then*

TRUSTING THE ONE WHO MAKES IT HAPPEN

Isn't it interesting how there are certain moments in one's life that stand out like a bright light? One of those amazingly memorable moments is locked in my brain as though it happened yesterday. Several years ago, after a Women of Faith conference in Sacramento, California, a group of us were going to dinner in the hotel restaurant as we often do on Saturday night. One of our editors was visiting that weekend, and I was eager to see her, bring her up to date on a project I'd been working on, and visit with her over our meal. I was rooming with Mary Graham that weekend and said to her just prior to leaving the room, "Mary, I'm not doing very well. I don't know what's wrong, but I feel sort of dizzy and light-headed. And, my heart is racing. For some reason it feels like it's gonna fly out of my body." She was very sweet, asking if I thought it was too much to have dinner after just having spoken at the conference. Should we cancel, or would I like to stay in the room and she would "represent me" with my friends and the visiting editor? "No, I'm okay to go, I think. I'm just not quite myself." I didn't want to be a party pooper, so I went downstairs to meet the rest of our gang, all the while thinking I'd just greet everybody, eat hurriedly, then come back up to the room.

As we were ordering dinner, I could barely see the words on the menu and told the person next to me I felt like I needed to lie down. In no time, I found myself on the floor of the restaurant, stretched out on my back, and I could hear someone over me praying aloud and someone else calling 911. Next, I was on a gurney and rolled out of there, into the back of an ambulance. Mary jumped in the front seat with the driver, and off we went. I could hear sirens screaming as I rode along in this out-of-body experience. I later learned, that others in our party followed the ambulance. Clearly, everyone was very concerned. I was immediately taken to a hospital emergency room. After an examination by the ER doctor, it was determined I had atrial fibrillation with rapid ventricular response. Who knew? I'd never even heard of it! I spent three days and nights in the hospital and had expert care.

During that time I was examined over and over and went through a battery of tests until the atrial fib finally converted itself into proper sinus rhythm (normal heartbeat).

When I entered the hospital I had no way of knowing if my health was in danger or if this was something simply related to hypertension. I'd been working very hard on a project that had a deadline, which I was trying desperately to meet. Maybe I was just terribly tired. However, my mother had died of heart arrest at the age of sixty-three, and my younger brother had had a heart attack at the age of sixty-eight. And here I was—at age seventy— with something weird going on in my heart. I was completely in the hands of God, and there was nowhere else to turn except to him. Even though I was surrounded by competent medical personnel, I knew life and death lay in the hands of my heavenly Father. I well remember one of the doctors ordered a procedure early Sunday morning that would determine if I had a blockage to my heart. Mary Graham was still with me in the room when they rolled me out to the examination area, and she was permitted to stay with me for that procedure. She sat on the foot of my gurney looking in the opposite direction to hide her tears, and I heard her ask softly, "Are you afraid, Luci?"

I thought for a minute and then answered. "Actually, I'm not. I don't know why I'm not, but I have peace. I know the Lord is with me, and I trust him. I belong to him, and I believe he'll take care of me." Even as I spoke those words out loud in that unfamiliar situation, I believed them with every fiber of my being. I knew they were true. My life was in his hands.

Those words came from a deep place inside me that was based on all I had learned through the years of what the Bible teaches about God the Father. When I thought about it in retrospect, I realized I did know why I was not afraid. It was because I was running that experience through the principles of my belief system. It was because I had a sound doctrinal core. Remember, John 16:30 says:

The Father is with me. I've told you all this so that trusting me, you will be unshakable and assured, deeply at peace. (MSG)

Something inside me was unshakable. I had no idea what was going to be the outcome, and had I known, I couldn't have done anything about it anyway . . . but the trust made my feelings unshakable. In Hebrews 10:31 it's explained even better:

Anyone who is right with me thrives on loyal trust. (MSG)

I had too much history with God for him not to meet me where I was in that hospital, and I knew it. I had enough biblical doctrine under my belt to know he was right there with me. His part of that experience was being faithful, and my part was to trust his faithfulness. It's as simple as that. He was in control. He loves me and has every area of my life covered. Regardless of the circumstances, I can rely on God.

There's a wonderful verse of scripture, Romans 1:17, which says, "The person in right standing before God by trusting him really lives" (MSG). Think about the power that comes when we believe that verse. If we want to really live, it means we must be in right standing before God by trusting him. What does it mean to trust God? What is trust, anyway? I looked it up in the dictionary. The word *trust* means to rely with certainty and assurance upon the integrity of one in whom confidence and authority are placed, with no fear of consequences. *With no fear of consequences.* Don't miss that part. It means to believe and expect steadfast honesty from the one in whom we've put our faith. Trust implies instinctive, unquestioning belief. If this verse is true (and it is), and if I want to "really live" (and I do), I need to trust God with everything about my life—my health, relationships, finances, work, commitments, reputation—past, present, and future. Regardless of changing circumstances at any given moment, I must put my confidence in him and not in myself. That is huge—and it's hard. But, it works. I must trust him when my heart is beating regularly as well as when it's out of whack. Being in a hospital is a perfect testing ground for trust, because one's very life is on the line.

Why is trusting God so hard? Jesus assures us that he will give us peace when we trust him. Look again at what he says through the pen of the apostle John:

The Father is with me. I've told you all this so that trusting me, you will be unshakable and assured, deeply at peace." (John 16:30–31 MSG)

Perhaps the reason trusting is so hard for us as human beings is because we try to understand the truth of these scriptures through our emotions rather than through the principles of our belief system. Remember, as Marilyn Meberg says, "emotions don't have brains," even though there are times we depend on what we feel more than depending on what we know. As I said in chapter 10, "Building a Foundation on Truth," we need a doctrinal platform on which to stand so we're not thrown a curve ball by our feelings, which may be the total opposite of what we *know for sure*. When our response to a problem is determined solely by what we feel, we run the chance of losing our spiritual footing. I'm not saying feelings are wrong; I'm saying they shouldn't be the only measurement by which we make decisions.

It's so interesting to me how God uses us in spite of ourselves. The farther down the road I go with him, the more I recognize he's in *everything* I do, think, and plan. I don't always know it or see it until it's over, but the hand of God is there, nevertheless. Because I belong to him and trust his sovereignty, I know for a fact that he is working in my needs, yearnings, stubbornness, fears, and heartaches, and in my inability to decide . . . or to cope. He's in it all. And he proves himself faithful and ever-present.

For example, just recently the Lord put an interesting test in front of me with money. First, read this verse in Malachi 3:10:

"Bring the whole tithe into the storehouse, that there may be food in my house. Test me in this," says the LORD *Almighty, "and see if I will not throw open the floodgates of heaven and pour out so much blessing that you will not have room enough for it."*

Here's what happened:

I was talking with Austin Gutwein (the fourteen-year-old founder of Hoops of Hope) not long ago when we were both on the bus on the way to the airport after a Revolve conference. I love this kid and think he's one in a million when it comes to a ministry of love and outreach. It's interesting that God brought us together to become close friends with such a huge age difference between us. Sometimes I laugh out loud at God and his mysterious but exceedingly clever ways.

The Hoops of Hope organization has raised a million dollars to help orphaned children in Zambia, and they continue to bring in money for schools, hospitals, housing, and other needs for these kids who have nobody to care for them.

On our ride to the airport, I was telling Austin about a set of books I wanted to buy. "They're called *Vincent van Gogh: The Letters*, and they've just been published. Came out October 7. Golly, I'd love to have those. Fifteen years of research went into that project. Can you imagine?"

"Why don't you get them, Miss Swindoll? They sound wonderful."

I told him the main reason is because they're so bloomin' expensive. "They're six hundred bucks, Austin. That's a lot of money. But I looked on Amazon, and they're selling that set for $480, which is a little better. I'd have to preorder them, but that's okay." I explained to Austin that I had seen the original letters at the Van Gogh Museum in Amsterdam and loved them. I wanted a set for my library. "There are nine hundred in all with over four thousand illustrations. Most of them were written to Theo, Vincent's brother, but there are others nobody's ever seen. They're fascinating." Austin asked why they cost so much. "Because those books are a work of art themselves. It's a six-volume set in a slipcase. Really great books."

He was listening very attentively when he suddenly said, "I think you ought to get them, Miss Swindoll."

"Well, here's the problem. I'm torn. God told me to give *you* the money, Austin. For Hoops for Hope."

"Of," he said. "Hoops *of* Hope."

We laughed about that for a minute, and then I said, "You know, Austin. I really, really want those books, but I feel like if the Lord tells me to give the money to somebody, I should do it. And, if I give you money, I don't want it to be $480. I think it should at least be $500. If I give you less, it feels a little cheesy. You know what I mean?"

"Yeah, I know what you mean." We sat silent for a while. I wasn't talking because I didn't know quite what else to say, and he wasn't talking because he's too much of a gentleman to ask for the money. So there we sat.

Finally, I said, " Austin, I'm gonna write you a check for $500 right now because I won't be able to live with myself if God is prompting me to do this and I don't do it. I'll feel like I blew an opportunity to really help Hoops for Hope. I don't want to blow it."

"Of," he said. "It's Hoops *of* Hope."

"Oh yeah. I forgot." Then I wrote him the check for $500 just as he was getting off the bus to go catch his flight.

As he was climbing over the seat and thanking me, he said, "I'll bet you have a surprise in your mailbox when you get home. God is going to give this money back to you, Miss Swindoll. When we give of ourselves or our money, he always rewards us somehow. You can test him, you know. It says so in Malachi 3. Check it out."

As the bus pulled away, I thought, *Gee I love that kid. So sharp and fun, and caring about other people. May his tribe increase!*

I got home. and the next day there was no surprise in my mailbox. I told the Lord that was okay—completely okay, because I trusted him totally. I was glad I had given the money to Austin. The next day, no surprise either. The week went on that way. But over the weekend, the surprise came. I unexpectedly received a check for five thousand dollars, paid to me for some work I had done for friends. I had no idea I would be getting that money. I stared at that check and thought, *Lord, you're the best!* Nobody can second-guess you or outdo you. You're full of surprises and provisions. You can pull money right out of the clouds. I love that about you. Thank you. *Thank you.*"

Then I called Austin on his cell phone. When he answered, I said, "Guess what, Austin? You're not going to believe this. I got a surprise in my mailbox and it was ten times more than what I gave you last week. Is that fabulous or what?"

"Oh. My. Gosh. That is *unreal*," he whispered as he was walking into a prayer meeting for a Revolve conference. "I can't wait to tell everybody. This is incredible."

"God really honors Hoops for Hope, Austin."

"Of," he said. "Hoops *of* Hope, Miss Swindoll." We both roared with laughter.

Austin is the youngest speaker for the Revolve Tour team, which is part of Thomas Nelson Live Events. And I'm the oldest speaker with Women of Faith. But it doesn't matter how young or old we are, does it? Austin is fifteen and I'm seventy-seven, yet we're on the same path, heading in the same direction, toward the same goal. I wouldn't take anything for my relationship with this young man. He's even written a book for Thomas Nelson now, called *Take Your Best Shot,* which his publisher asked me to endorse. "With pleasure," I said. "I'd do anything for that boy. I love him. If he were taller, I'd marry him."

As I come to the close of this book, I can't help thinking about my mother. In many ways, it was she who taught me to trust the Lord. She introduced my two brothers and me to Christ when we were children and even though she's been in glory for almost forty years, there's hardly a day that goes by I don't think of her. In some ways, she drove me crazy. By nature, Mother was moody, artistic, controlling . . . yet wonderful. We rarely knew how she was going to be when she got up in the morning. Having a capricious temperament made her unpredictable, but God used that to help me lean on him all the more, as well as become closer and closer to my father. Daddy helped me understand Mother because he loved her so much. When I wanted to give up or run away from home, Daddy listened to my heart and sympathized with my impatience—all the while continuing to love Mother dearly. He let me rant and rave. He received me just as I was, just as I felt. He understood the petulant child in me. When I realized this at such an early age, I pictured God to be just like Daddy—loving, kind, patient, and trustworthy. So through my mother's omission and my father's commission, I learned to deal with the vagaries of life in the long haul. I learned to trust God because he's the only One who can make things happen. It's not my mother or father in whom I've put my trust. It's not my siblings. It's not my friends or coworkers. It's not my peers. It's God.

Sometimes, the hardest thing in the world is to trust God. It requires letting go of my preference and waiting on him to lead. But that's how I'd like to live the rest of my days on earth. I want to be able to deal with the changes that come with aging. I want to have the coping skills required to take me to the end. Who knows how many years I have left? Nobody. But I know the one in whom I have put my trust, and it is he who matters the most.

I'm not going to quit doing life differently as long as I'm alive and kickin'. So what if I am tired or cranky? Who cares if I have to make adjustments? Life isn't easy for anyone, so why should my problems have a simple solution? As long as I have children to sponsor, friends like Austin, a platform from which to encourage others and give the gospel, I have a job to do, and I'm going to get out there and do it. All of us have crises in our lives, including me. But more often than not, we learn they really aren't crises at all. They're simply life, the ebb and flow of God bringing us to maturity.

Won't you join me in capturing the difference in life by developing the best in yourself and trusting the God you love to make that happen?

God, the one and only—I'll wait as long as he says. Everything I need comes from him, so why not? He's solid rock under my feet, breathing room for my soul, an impregnable castle: I'm set for life. (Psalm 62:1–2 MSG)

How willing am I to be totally myself, and what will it cost me?

The Bible is an amazing volume of work—like no other!

_____
_____
_____
_____
_____
_____
_____
_____
_____
_____
_____
_____
_____
_____
_____
_____
_____
_____

The greater the trust, the wider the blessing.
The wider the blessing, the sweeter the joy.

We need an advocate to go before us as well as run with us. Someone who will fight our battles and cheer us on. Someone who will forgive us and strengthen us for the next task. This person is the Savior, Jesus Christ . . . God and man in one person forever.

_____

_____

_____

_____

_____

_____

_____

_____

_____

_____

_____

_____

_____

_____

_____

_____

_____

_____

_____

Notes

1. Henry Wadsworth Longfellow, *The Poetic Works* (Boston and New York: Houghton, Mifflin and Company, 1882), 27.
2. Sara Teasdale, *Collected Poems of Sara Teasdale* (New York: Macmillan Co.), 102.
3. Francis Thompson, *The Hound of Heaven* (Mount Vernon, NY: Peter Pauper Press, 1912), 11–12.
4. Used by permission of Jason Lehman.
5. Hermann Hesse, *Klingsor's Last Summer* (New York: Farrar, Straus and Giroux, 1971), 167.
6. Pindar, "Human Life," in *The Oxford Book of Greek Verse in Translation* (Oxford: Clarendon Press, 1958), 312.
7. Robert Henri, *The Art Spirit* (Philadelphia and New York: J. B. Lippincott Company, 1923), 13.
8. William Shakespeare, *Hamlet*, act 1, scene 3 in *Complete Works* (Oxford: Oxford University Press, 1987), 875.
9. Robert MacNeil, *Wordstruck* (New York: Viking Penguin, Inc., 1989), 23–24.
10. Hesse, *Klingsor's Last Summer*, 166.
11. Rupert Brooke, *The Collected Poems of Rupert Brooke* (New York: Dodd, Mead and Company, 1963), 153.
12. Milan Kundera, *The Unbearable Lightness of Being* (New York: Harper and Row Publishers, Inc., 1984), 297.
13. Kazantzakis, *Report to Greco*, 477.
14. John Donne, *The Poems of John Donne* (Norwalk, CT: Easton Press, 1979), 190–91.
15. Charles L. Swindoll, ed., *The Living Insights Bible* (Grand Rapids, MI: Zondervan Publishing House, 1996), 1290.
16. Kazantzakis, *Report to Greco*, 276.
17. Howard Shultz, *Pour Your Heart Into It* (New York: Hyperion, 1999), 337.
18. Leo Buscaglia, *Bus Nine to Paradise* (New York: William Morrow, 1986).
19. Simone Weil, *Gateway to God*, trans. David Raper, with Malcolm Muggeride and Vernon Sproxton (London: Fontana, 1974).
20. Henry W. Baker, words: "The King of Love My Shepherd Is," *Hymns Ancient and Modern*, 1868.

Acknowledgments

Before closing the final page in this book, please allow me to express my thanks to those who have made this publication possible. The idea for the book first came up when I was traveling with Stephen Arterburn and his wife on a trip to India in 2001. While there he encouraged me to read a book titled *I Married Adventure*, written by Osa Johnson in 1940.

Johnson wrote the book as a tribute to her photojournalist husband Martin after he was killed in a plane crash. It's a wonderful account of her life with Martin and the details of their adventures, curiosities, problems, daring and fun. In fact, *National Geographic* names it as one of the best adventure books of all time. I would have to agree.

Stephen then encouraged me to write about my own adventures and how they had shaped my life—what resulted was my own *I Married Adventure*, published in 2002. And now, drawing close to a decade later, I have been able to revise and add new material to the first fifteen chapters and incorporate it into *Doing Life Differently*.

Not only has it been exciting to bring all these thoughts and stories together, but the challenge of doing so has made me realize again and again there's no way I could have done it without certain people, to whom I owe a huge debt of gratitude. In particular, I think of Mary Graham, who constantly encouraged me, when I KNEW I could never get the manuscript written on time (but I did); Tami Heim, who clarified the purpose behind the need for such a book when I didn't think it mattered (but she did); and Vance Lawson, who served as my advocate in difficult circumstances when I wanted to quit (but he kept rooting for me). These three friends should have additional stars in their crowns one day because of their sheer kindness to and patience with me during those hard days.

I don't want to forget David Riley, who designed the original book—straight out of his fertile imagination—and gave great attention to all the details that make it unique and artistic. I've known David since he was about seven, and he had a very creative mind then. But NOW he has become a genius. So, my thanks to him . . . and the designers who have followed in his footsteps to make the book what it is today.

And finally, my sincere appreciation to the people at the Thomas Nelson Publishing Group who have worked diligently to bring everything to completion in a timely manner. In particular, I want to commend Brian Hampton, Susan Hagenau, and Bryan Norman for their collective efforts in keeping things on track. I know that editing is not always an easy, enjoyable task . . . so many thanks for the labor that was extended to this project on my behalf. I trust as you look back on our working together, you will do so with joy.